Environmental Groups

Look for these and other books in the Lucent Overview Series:

Acid Rain
Advertising
Animal Rights
Cancer
Cities
Democracy
Elections
Endangered Species
Energy Alternatives
Garbage
The Greenhouse Effect
Hazardous Waste
Ocean Pollution
Oil Spills
Ozone
Pesticides
Population
Poverty
Rainforests
Recycling
Vanishing Wetlands

Environmental Groups

by Patricia D. Netzley

LUCENT
BOOKS

LUCENT *Overview Series*

LUCENT *Overview Series*

With thanks to Raymond, Matthew, Sarah,
and Jacob Netzley; Marge and George Faber; Eleanor Morgan;
Brenda Ulyate; and Andrea Brown

Library of Congress Cataloging-in-Publication Data

Netzley, Patricia D.
    Environmental groups / by Patricia D. Netzley.
        p.   cm. — (Lucent overview series)
    Includes bibliographical references and index.
    Summary: Examines the history, tactics, and effectiveness of
various grassroots and national level environmental groups, as well as
the state of the environment and the economic costs of protecting it.
    ISBN 1-56006-195-2 (lib. bdg. : alk. paper)
    1. Environmentalists—Juvenile literature.   2. Environmentalism
—Juvenile literature.   3. Social groups—Juvenile literature.
[1. Environmental protection.   2. Environmentalists.]   I. Title.
II. Series.
GE80.N48   1998
363.7'0525—dc21   98-12735
                                                              CIP
                                                              AC

Copyright © 1998 by Lucent Books, Inc.
P.O. Box 289011, San Diego, CA 92198-9011
Printed in the U.S.A.

Contents

INTRODUCTION   6

CHAPTER ONE   11
The Changing Face of Environmental Groups

CHAPTER TWO   22
The Tactics of Modern Environmental Groups

CHAPTER THREE   34
Assessing the True State of the Environment

CHAPTER FOUR   44
Economic Issues and Opposition Movements

CHAPTER FIVE   60
New Forms of Environmentalism

ORGANIZATIONS TO CONTACT   73
SUGGESTIONS FOR FURTHER READING   79
WORKS CONSULTED   81
INDEX   91
PICTURE CREDITS   95
ABOUT THE AUTHOR   96

Introduction

THOUSANDS OF ENVIRONMENTAL groups exist
to address environmental problems. Some are small grassroots groups run by volunteers. Others are large national or
international mainstream groups staffed by salaried em-
ployees. Grassroots groups work primarily on local problems; most struggle for the money and members to achieve
their goals. Mainstream groups work on national or global
problems and hire professionals to supervise successful
fund-raising and membership drives.

Not surprisingly, the budgets of the largest mainstream
groups far surpass those of grassroots groups. The twenty-
five largest organizations receive about 70 percent of the
$500 to $700 million that Americans donate to environmental groups each year. They use these funds to buy advertising, publish books, and promote media events to
disseminate their environmental views. They also sponsor
environmental programs and scientific research, pay
lawyers to fight for environmental laws and regulations,
and hire lobbyists to influence political decisions on environmental issues.

Widespread but qualified popular support

All of these activities have brought about significant
changes in the way Americans view the environment and
environmental protection, and many people applaud environmental groups for their accomplishments. In his book *A
Moment on the Earth*, environmental reporter Gregg Easterbrook states:

Because of the success of political environmentalism, Americans and Europeans today live in a world where effective environmental influence is assured at nearly every level of government and business. This is a wonderful development for society. History will admire the environmentalists of our era for how much they accomplished and how fast.

Easterbrook appears to hold the majority opinion. Environmental reporter Mark Dowie, in his book *Losing Ground: American Environmentalism at the Close of the Twentieth Century*, cites several surveys that indicate most people support environmentalism. Approximately 80 percent of Americans call themselves environmentalists, and 82 percent believe that more could be done to protect the environment. However, when environmentalism is discussed in terms of its expense, the number of supporters declines. In a recent *New York Times* poll, only 45 percent of respondents agreed that "protecting the environment is so important that requirements and standards cannot be too high and continuing environmental improvements must be made regardless of cost."

Approximately 80 percent of Americans consider themselves environmentalists. Here, protesters march in Washington, D.C., at a "Save the Forests" rally in 1990.

This finding indicates that many people believe environmental groups promote policies that are too expensive. Dixy Lee Ray, a former assistant secretary of the U.S. Bureau of the Oceans, and reporter Lou Guzzo severely criticize environmental groups for ignoring the economic impact of environmentalism. In *Environmental Overkill: Whatever Happened to Common Sense?* Ray and Guzzo maintain that environmental laws, regulations, and programs should be enacted only if they are "appropriate, practical, and affordable":

> In the name of environmentalism, it is no longer enough to be kind to animals, careful of wastes, and sensitive to ecosystems. According to the spokesmen for the environmental movement (those who are leaders and officers of the large international

organizations . . .), it is necessary not only to be good stewards of the Earth and its resources, but it is essential also to reduce human impact upon the air, water, and land, and to do it immediately by any and all means possible—no matter how drastic, no matter how costly. This extreme view of environmentalism is, unfortunately, the one that drives public policy.

Challenges to environmentalist motivation

Ray and Guzzo also suggest that environmentalists often propose solutions to environmental problems on the basis of

emotion rather than fact. They condemn environmental groups for taking action on environmental issues without scientific support for their positions: "Billions of dollars have been wasted on precipitous actions that weren't necessary, instances where political action moved faster than scientific research justified, and where government bureaucrats and the public just plain overreacted."

Other critics suggest that environmental groups allow not only emotion but money to influence their decisions. For example, Mark Dowie criticizes mainstream groups for allowing fund-raising potential to set their agendas. He points out that 65 to 70 percent of their revenue comes from millions of small donors as opposed to a few wealthy individuals or corporations, which means that main-

In protest of toxic waste, a man wears a protective yellow coat at an environmental demonstration. Many environmentalists are criticized for acting out of emotion for their causes despite scientific fact.

stream groups are dependent on public opinion. Consequently, mainstream groups tend to promote popular causes that "often don't go to the heart of the organization's mission or even to the requisites for a healthy environment."

Environmentalist Dave Foreman also criticizes mainstream environmental groups for allowing fund-raising considerations to set their agendas. But he believes that politics are equally to blame for destroying the groups' objectivity. In his book *Confessions of an Eco-Warrior*, he writes that mainstream environmentalists often have "a higher loyalty to the political process than to conservation," adding: "Some have strong personal loyalties to particular political figures, loyalties that often override commitment to protection of wilderness or enhancement of environmental quality. Certain politicians . . . are placed on a pedestal and are not intensively . . . criticized."

Dissatisfied with environmental politics, Foreman established one of the first so-called radical environmental groups. Members of such groups believe that conservative approaches to environmentalism are ineffective. Instead they promote confrontational activism, physically blocking or secretly sabotaging any project that threatens to harm the environment or plant or animal populations. In their attempts to protect the earth, they sometimes break laws or commit violent acts.

As a result, radical environmentalism is not popular with the American public. Mark Dowie reports on a survey by a radical environmental group, Greenpeace, that revealed: "Of the several million people out there who might become supporting members of the organization, very few were impressed with direct confrontation as a tactic—even when it worked in the struggle against environmental adversaries." Moreover, people donate less money to groups they perceive as confrontational.

Therefore, both mainstream and grassroots groups have worked hard to distance themselves from their radical counterparts, criticizing such organizations in public. At the same time, mainstream and grassroots groups openly quarrel with one another about which approaches to environmentalism are best. Mainstream groups say that while grassroots groups are helpful, they are not very important or effective at the national level, while grassroots groups complain that mainstream groups are arrogant and insensitive to problems at the local level.

Reinvigorating a fragmented movement

Mark Dowie sees such infighting as counterproductive. He believes that divisiveness within the environmental

Surveys suggest that the American public prefers environmental efforts that are less radical and confrontational. This group of radical protesters handcuffed themselves to a truck outside the White House to protest hazardous waste.

community is damaging the environmental movement as a whole, and suggests that all groups need to embrace a common vision. However, he believes that no such vision currently exists. He thinks that a new form of environmentalism will have to be developed, one that recaptures the passion of an earlier time and combines it with a modern approach to environmental issues:

> If American environmentalism is to remain a vital force in the next century it will be because its leaders return to the fundamentals of the original movement, recoup some of the passion lost during the previous three decades, and create a dynamic working vision of environmental recovery.

Many other critics agree that environmental groups have strayed far from their original purpose. Mainstream groups in particular have changed a great deal since their formation, and many critics believe that these changes have diminished their effectiveness. In order to understand why, it is necessary to trace the history of these groups and examine their philosophical differences.

1

The Changing Face of Environmental Groups

IN THE LATE 1800s, environmentalists were called conservationists, and most nature-related groups had little wealth or political power. These early environmental groups were actually small, regional clubs devoted to hunting or other forms of wilderness enjoyment. As Wallace Kaufman explains in his book *No Turning Back:* "The conservation movement began as the 'club movement.' The clubs were formed after the Civil War by men who hunted and fished for recreation."

Kaufman reports that at some point nineteenth-century hunters and fishermen soon decided to dedicate their clubs to conserving the natural resources they so enjoyed:

> Issues that today seem to have been brought to the public by the environmental movement were made hot topics a century ago by sportsmen. They protested industrial chemicals and mining waste that polluted streams and lakes. They attacked commercial net fishing and clear-cutting of watersheds. They sponsored scientific research on fish breeding and restocking. Sportsmen began tagging fish to trace their life cycles as early as 1896.

The Audubon Society

One of the oldest and largest mainstream environmental groups formed by conservationists is the Audubon Society, founded in 1886 in response to fears that certain species of plumed birds would soon become extinct. These birds were being wantonly hunted for their feathers, which were a fashionable decoration on hats, belts, purses, and clothing at the time.

The early organizers of the Audubon Society included John Bird Grinnell, an outdoorsman and expert on Native American cultures; William Dutcher, an insurance agent whose hobby was bird hunting; and a group of Boston women upset by the slaughter of feathered birds. They named the society after John James Audubon, an early-nineteenth-century American ornithologist and artist who had catalogued over 435 species of birds, whom Grinnell wished to honor posthumously. Audubon's wife, Lucy, had been Grinnell's elementary school teacher.

Together the group's amateur conservationists built the Audubon Society into a major organization, and in 1905 they rechristened it the National Audubon Society. In the beginning this new organization worked primarily at the state level, but in the 1950s it broadened its scope to include national issues. However, its main focus remained the protection of birds from overhunting.

From conservation to environmentalism

Then in the early 1960s this focus changed. In 1962 biologist Rachel Carson published a controversial book, *Silent Spring*, which exposed the destructive environmental effects of chemical pesticides, especially DDT, then in widespread use. Carson maintained that these chemicals, ingested by birds and animals higher up the food chain, had the potential to cause cancer in human beings. Her book wedded fact and emotional appeal to create a convincing argument against the careless poisoning of air, land, and water.

Silent Spring deeply affected the American public. Robert Gottlieb, in his book *Forcing the Spring*, explains:

> The book received enormous attention from politicians and policy makers as well as scientists and had a wide and passionate following among the public. . . . [Carson] strongly countered her critics by continuing to elaborate the key ele-

ments of her argument [which included the concepts] that science could be purchased and thus corrupted; that the rise of pesticides was indicative of "an era dominated by industry, in which the right to make money, at whatever cost to others, is seldom challenged"; and that the pesticide problem revealed how hazardous technologies could pollute both natural and human environments.

The Audubon Society responded to *Silent Spring* by becoming one of the first major conservation groups to embrace the new environmental movement that followed the publication of Carson's book. According to Gottlieb: "The group was most absorbed by the pesticide issue, particularly in light of the controversies concerning *Silent Spring* and pressure within the organization to pursue a more forceful role against [the pesticide] DDT."

The campaign against DDT

In fact, the Audubon Society had been concerned about the effect of DDT on birds even before *Silent Spring*. Several disturbing incidents had already been reported about DDT, which was developed as an insecticide but seemed to be killing birds as well.

Gottlieb explains that in the late 1950s, when pesticides were widely sprayed on forests and roadsides to combat mosquitoes, "enough fish and birds were being killed and farmworkers poisoned to cast doubt on industry and government claims about the pesticide revolution. These problems . . . led to some initial protests against spraying campaigns, including a DDT-related lawsuit filed on Long Island [New York]."

Once the Audubon Society recognized the serious damage to bird populations that DDT caused, it turned from conservationism to environmentalism. This new direction brought many changes within the organization. According to

Author Rachel Carson created a stir in 1962 when her controversial book Silent Spring *exposed the dangers of chemical pesticides.*

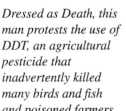

Dressed as Death, this man protests the use of DDT, an agricultural pesticide that inadvertently killed many birds and fish and poisoned farmers.

Gottlieb, between 1968 and 1978, "Audubon hired a number of staff scientists, increased its lobbying presence in Washington, initiated direct-mail solicitation on specific environmental topics, and restructured its main publication, *Audubon*, to reflect a broader interest in environmental or ecology themes." In other words, the Audubon Society began to employ lobbyists, who work to influence decisions within the legislative and executive branches of the U.S. government, and to concern itself with environmental issues not directly related to birds.

Not all of the group's members were comfortable with this new approach to bird conservation. Gottlieb says that "membership unease with the transition was most forcefully expressed by those who felt the organization should remain 'synonymous with birds and birding' and not environmental advocacy, as one member wrote [in *Audubon* magazine]." Nonetheless, the Audubon Society continued to expand its scope, defending this decision by claiming it would benefit birds. The group's on-line literature currently states:

> Rooted in more than a century of activism on behalf of birds, today's National Audubon Society maintains the traditions of our founders. But just as threats to birds have evolved, so have our methods of effecting change on their behalf. No longer are we fighting the hunters of commerce. Today, threats to birds are less direct and more complicated: habitat loss, pesticides, pollution, booming population, increased development, water management, and technology are among the most severe.

To combat these problems, the modern Audubon Society works to educate the public about conservation issues. They also manage bird sanctuaries and operate conservation programs. But more importantly, they work within the

American legal system to change environmental policies, particularly those relating to bird habitats such as ancient forests and wetlands.

With over 570,000 members and an annual budget of approximately $42 million, the Audubon Society has ample resources to file lawsuits related to environmental concerns. They are no longer a small group devoted to a particular bird-related problem. Instead they address a wide range of environmental issues at the national level.

The Sierra Club

Most of the early mainstream environmental groups have undergone similar transitions. In moving from conservationism to environmentalism, they have learned to use legal tactics to achieve their increasingly broad goals. Some of them, like the Sierra Club, rely more heavily on litigation than others.

The Sierra Club is a national organization that currently has over 550,000 members. With a 1994 annual income of

An ornithologist with the Audubon Society works on a puffin conservation project in Maine. The Audubon Society manages many bird sanctuaries and strives to educate the public about conservation efforts.

approximately $41 million, it is one of the five wealthiest environmental groups in America and has ample resources to file lawsuits. However, like the Audubon Society, it originally began as a small club with a single purpose: to promote recreational hiking in California's Sierra Nevada.

The club was founded in 1892 by the American naturalist John Muir, who had helped establish Yosemite National Park 1890. Yosemite was even in Muir's time a showpiece of the Sierra Nevada, and Muir wanted others to enjoy and appreciate the wilderness he loved. He wrote ten major books and more than three hundred articles promoting his naturalist philosophy and encouraging people to value outdoor activities.

Theodore Roosevelt stands with naturalist John Muir on Glacier Point overlooking Yosemite Valley in California. Muir founded the Sierra Club in 1892.

Muir's focus was wilderness recreation, and the early activities of the Sierra Club reflected this. In 1901 the Sierra Club began to promote hiking expeditions in other parts of the country besides California. But Muir also wanted to educate the public, so these expeditions typically had an educational aspect. Along the trail, biologists, geologists, and other scientists often gave lectures about nature and the environment.

Public education remains a strong part of the Sierra Club's agenda today, but like the Audubon Society, the group changed other aspects of its agenda when certain environmental dangers became apparent. For example, after it realized that wilderness areas were being damaged by human use, the Sierra Club decided to limit its promotion of recreational activities. In 1951 its board of directors changed the group's statement of purpose, replacing the words "explore, enjoy, and render accessible" with "explore, enjoy, and preserve" in regards to wilderness areas. This emphasis on preservation triggered the

Sierra Club's increasing reliance on legal tactics. The Sierra Club currently files many environmental lawsuits on both the federal and local levels.

The NRDC and the Alliance for Justice

The Sierra Club underwent a transition to legal activism; some of the more recent mainstream environmental groups were formed specifically for that purpose. For example, the Natural Resources Defense Council (NRDC) was founded in 1970 to promote environmental litigation. Its members include such prominent attorneys as Robert F. Kennedy Jr., and it has been involved in numerous environmental lawsuits.

In fact, according to the *Wall Street Journal:* "It's hard to find a major environmental law NRDC hasn't helped shape within Congress, the courts and federal agencies and often, the influence is profound." The NRDC quotes David H. Getches, a professor at the University of Colorado School of Law:

> Look in the books we use to teach environmental law. You will find at least seven major cases NRDC took to the United States Supreme Court, as well as landmark cases in every branch of environmental law, litigated in all of the federal and state courts. If a law student is asked in a class discussion of almost any environmental law issue, "What case established that principle?" he or she would be wise to guess, "Um, I think it was the NRDC case." In the leading law school environmental law treatise, there are fifty-five cases named NRDC.

Today the NRDC has 350,000 members nationwide and relies heavily on the American political system as well as legal tactics to achieve its goals. Its association with Kennedy, son of the famous American political family, reflects its connection to political activism.

In recent years, more and more environmental groups have begun to view political activism as a necessary component of environmentalism. They often turn to political organizations like the Alliance for Justice to learn the tactics of political activism.

The Alliance for Justice is an association of environmental, civil rights, consumer, and women's organizations that offers advice regarding public-interest law and political activism. It counsels its members on voter education and registration as well as political lobbying. It sponsors a judicial selection project, which disseminates information about judges and judicial nominees at the federal level, and helps environmental groups comply with the federal government's Lobbying Disclosure Act of 1995. This law, which became effective on January 1, 1996, establishes new reporting requirements for certain organizations that use lobbyists.

Attorney Robert F. Kennedy Jr., pictured here in 1990, is a member of the Natural Resources Defense Council, which helps fight for environmental issues in the legal arena.

Grassroots groups

Mainstream environmental groups rely heavily on political activism to achieve their environmental goals. However, grassroots environmental groups, which work on local issues, often disapprove of the form this political activism takes at the national level. They complain that mainstream groups are too eager to make compromises to get a law passed, without considering how those compromises will affect individual communities. In *Losing Ground*, Mark Dowie quotes Kate Crockett, an Alaskan grassroots activist:

> An environmental problem arises locally. People work to address the problem, develop a solution—frequently legislative—and gather support. As soon as the bill reaches [Washington] D.C.—or sometimes the state capital—a national group comes in and with lobbying power and money takes over the issue and cuts a deal to pass the bill. They get the credit in the media *and* with the foundations. The grassroots lose in two ways. They don't get credit, and they are not at the [bargaining] table. . . . The reality is that there is always something to deal away in order to pass a bill. The grassroots are capable of determining what to trade, but when the deal is cut without them they see what they have lost and they don't own the decision.

There are thousands of grassroots groups in America. The first ones formed during the environmental movement, and new ones continue to appear today in response to local environmental problems, primarily as they relate to public health. Dowie explains:

> People are drawn to grassroots environmental politics because they fear for their lives and those of their children. Although they tend to be patriotic and conservative in most matters, they are generally suspicious of electoral politics, cynical about government, and wary of large organizations, no matter how civic minded and well meaning they may appear. Most would never have called themselves environmentalists before they were active, and some still refuse to do so. Their motivation is protection of family and neighborhood, although many develop an appreciation of traditional environmental goals—and even a global perspective—after joining the fray and meeting experts from the Natural Resources Defense Council, Greenpeace, and others who come to their assistance.

Grassroots groups primarily work on issues of pollution and toxic waste. They form to address a problem and generally disband either when that problem is solved or when volunteer support dies out. However, some groups gain strength through alliances with other grassroots groups. For example, during the 1980s, a group called the National Toxics Campaign Fund united thousands of grassroots groups, helping them share information and scientific research on various forms of pollution.

In 1990 this grassroots group in San Diego protested outside a McDonald's restaurant to ban the use of polystyrene products. At the time, McDonald's was the largest single user of polystyrene foam in the nation.

Radical environmentalists

Most mainstream and grassroots environmental groups use conventional legal and political tactics to solve environmental problems. However, radical environmental groups use legally questionable means to achieve their goals.

Earth First! activists often take a radical approach to spreading their environmental message. These Earth First!ers were arrested at the Lincoln Memorial in 1987 for protesting against rain forest destruction.

Radical environmental groups were not a part of the conservation movement that began with John Muir and others like him. Instead they appeared during the environmental movement of the 1960s, 1970s, and early 1980s. Founded by people who believe that mainstream environmental groups are ineffective, radical groups have a different approach to environmentalism. For example, the radical group Earth First!, established in 1980, shuns a traditional approach to environmentalism and calls itself a movement rather than an organization.

Today this attitude is reflected in the fact that Earth First! has no official members and no budget report. Its literature states: "Earth First! is not an organization but a movement. There are no members of Earth First!, only Earth First!ers." Earth First! is therefore more appropriately defined as a coalition of affiliated activists rather than a single environmental group, and most of its actions occur on the local level.

But this does not mean that the group does not have a national, unifying philosophy. In its literature, it criticizes mainstream environmental groups for being "more worried about their image than saving wilderness" and advocates a "hard-line position" mandating that "the Earth must come first." It promotes the idea that the environment should take precedence over the rights of human beings and says: "While there is a broad diversity within Earth First! . . . there is agreement on one thing: the need for action!"

How Earth First! and other radical environmental groups interpret this need for action is a controversial issue. Their activities are criticized by mainstream and grassroots environmental groups, which advocate a more conservative approach to environmentalism. Environmentalists do not agree on the appropriate tactics that should be used to achieve their goals, just as their critics do not agree on whether these goals are really worth achieving.

2

The Tactics of Modern Environmental Groups

MAINSTREAM, GRASSROOTS, and radical environmental groups operate very differently from one another. Mainstream groups work within the prevailing legal and political systems at the national level, influencing lawmakers, government officials, and the public to create new environmental laws, policies, and practices. Grassroots groups work at the local level to address specific environmental problems, using tactics similar to those of mainstream environmentalists. Radical groups work against the prevailing legal and political systems, often flouting the law and the government to fight what they call "anti-environmentalism."

Buying land

One of the primary goals of mainstream environmental groups is to maintain biodiversity, or the existing variety of biological species on Earth. Therefore they work to preserve wildlife habitats and support research on endangered plants and animals.

The main tactic that mainstream environmental groups use to protect a piece of property is to buy it outright. In fact, some groups have been established specifically for this purpose. For example, the Nature Conservancy was founded in 1946 by scientists interested in preserving ecosystems. At first the conservancy bought pieces of wilderness at random, but eventually it decided to concentrate only on pieces of property that harbored endangered plant and animal species. Today it is one of the wealthiest environmental groups in America, with an annual budget of approximately $278.49 million and a December 1995 membership of over 797,000. It protects approximately 6 million acres of land in the United States and, with the help of international partner organizations, approximately 22 million acres in other countries.

Litigation

Sometimes, however, a piece of property cannot be bought. In such cases, mainstream environmental groups turn to litigation to block land development. For example, in 1996 the Sierra Club filed a lawsuit against the city of Thousand Oaks, California, for granting a developer permission to build 584 homes on the former Dos Vientos Ranch. This is a small development, yet the Sierra Club believes it will cause a major problem.

According to a September 20, 1996, article in the *Los Angeles Times* by Miguel Bustillo, the ranch land at the

Jerry Barnett/*Indianapolis News*. Used with permission.

center of the dispute is one of only two wildlife corridors that allow bobcats, deer, and other mammals to travel between the Santa Monica and Santa Susana mountain ranges. Stephan C. Volker of the Sierra Club Legal Defense Fund insists: "If this project goes on as planned and you lose that corridor, we could see the end of large mammals in the Santa Monica Mountains in 50 to 200 years." Attorneys for the developer counter that there is no "corridor"; animals travel from mountain range to mountain range in many ways.

But Cassandra Auerbach, chairwoman of a Sierra Club chapter in the Thousand Oaks area, says that the Dos Vientos controversy shows that her city is "willing to sacrifice public interest and the public safety for developer's profits and long-term financial gain." She believes that lawsuits are an essential tool for environmental activism: "The days of careful planning are gone. Our only resource is through the courts."

Political efforts

An Earth Day volunteer works at an environmental petition table. Petitions are an important aspect of political activism because they help in the passage of environment-related laws.

When litigation fails to win protection for a piece of land, mainstream environmental groups often turn to political activism. By changing the laws related to land use, environmentalists can keep developers from destroying the habitats of endangered species.

In its simplest form, political activism is the support of a candidate who believes in environmental causes. Bill Green, cochair of a New Jersey Sierra Club chapter, offers an example of this in Elaine Landau's book *Environmental Groups: The Earth Savers:*

> One of [the Sierra Club's] main routes of protecting nature is through political action. We get people to write letters and explain how you can lobby effectively right in your home town where you have political representation. The Sierra Club does this on a national and state level as well as locally. There are a lot of politicians who'd like to have our vote.

In addition to letter writing and similar tactics, mainstream environmental groups express political support through campaign contributions. For example, the Sierra Club spent $7.5 million on the 1996 elections in the United States at the national and local levels. Most of this money went toward campaign advertising for or against candidates according to their environmental views.

Environmental groups are, however, subject to the same campaign-contribution limits imposed by Congress on all individuals or organizations. These limits are complicated, but according to professor of economics Filip Palda, essentially an individual or environmental group cannot give more than $1,000 directly to a candidate. However, an environmental group can set up an independent PAC, or political action committee, which can receive and distribute more money to candidates or political parties. In his article "How Cash Keeps Democracy Healthy," Palda explains:

> Individuals may contribute $5,000 to PACs. . . . PACs are like funnels. They ask the ordinary American for a contribution. They then either spend this contribution on political advertising or give the money directly to a sympathetic candidate or party. Almost every social and economic group in the United States has [a PAC]. Doctors, environmentalists, consumer groups . . . and thousands of others could not get their message across without setting up a PAC.

Grassroots differences

Mainstream environmental groups also influence the political process by hiring lobbyists. Lobbyists see their function as providing legislators with expert knowledge on the merits or faults of upcoming legislation, hoping to persuade lawmakers to vote in the interests of the lobbyists' clients. In the process, they sometimes make compromises.

The idea of compromising on environmental issues disturbs some people within the movement. In particular, grassroots environmental groups do not believe in sacrificing their ideals. As an example, in *Losing Ground* Mark Dowie reports that when one senator called the environmentalists "the most effective lobby in Washington" in 1985, "it was taken as a compliment by mainstreamers. To grassroots environmentalists, however, the Washington establishment began to look less like an idealistic social movement and more like a special interest group indistinguishable from the other 2,000 or so lobbies" in government that worked on other issues.

Dowie explains that grassroots groups are passionate about their beliefs because they are fighting for their own health and well-being. Because they primarily work to stop pollution and other environmental damage in their own communities, they have a personal stake in the outcome of government negotiations. Therefore, according to Dowie, "Grassroots organizations use many of the same tactics as mainstream groups—principally lobbying and negotiation—but they come to the table with an indignation that only a victim can display. Their anger and desperation are real and justifiable."

Monkeywrenching

Radical environmental groups also bring a great deal of passion to environmental issues. However, their focus and tactics are very different from grassroots groups. Whereas grassroots groups typically fight threats to human health, radical groups primarily deal with wilderness and animal protection issues. Moreover, while grassroots groups work within established legal and political systems, radical groups are willing to do almost anything to accomplish their goals.

Radical environmentalists argue that when a particular piece of land is threatened, it should be protected immediately. They believe that the needs of the earth take precedence over laws regarding property and land use. For example, the on-line literature of Earth First! in Manchester, England, states:

> Our motto is "No compromise in the defense of the Earth" and, above all, it is this uncompromising position that inspires the public, other environmentalists, and even our opponents. Earth First! has often been condemned by government and industry as radical extremists yet, time and time again, it has been our direct actions that have forced real discussion and real change. We believe in using all the tools in the tool

box, ranging from grassroots organizing and litigation to civil disobedience and monkeywrenching.

Monkeywrenching is an illegal form of activism. The term was first used in a 1975 novel by Edward Abbey entitled *The Monkey Wrench Gang*, which was based on true stories of guerrilla environmentalists in the southwestern United States during the late 1960s and early 1970s. Dave Foreman, one of the founders of Earth First!, defines the tactic as "ecological sabotage" or "ecodefense" that involves "the destruction of machines or property that are used to destroy the natural world." He adds that monkeywrenching is "nonviolent" because it is "aimed only at inanimate objects, *never* toward physically hurting people":

> [Monkeywrenching] is defensive in that it is used to prevent destructive development in wild places and in seminatural areas next to cities. . . . The goals of monkeywrenching are to block environmentally destructive projects, to increase the costs of such projects and thereby make them economically unattractive, and to raise public awareness of the taxpayer-subsidized devastation of biological diversity occurring throughout the world.

Serious consequences

Foreman portrays monkeywrenching as victimless harassment that "includes such acts as pulling up survey

Earth First! activists are sometimes criticized for their potentially violent monkeywrenching tactics.

stakes, putting sand in the crankcases of bulldozers, rendering dirt roads in wild areas impassable to vehicles, cutting down billboards, and removing and destroying trap lines." But critics of Earth First! point out that monkeywrenching has sometimes had serious consequences.

For example, in May 1987 a group of Earth First! monkeywrenchers hammered large metal nails, or spikes, deep into some trees marked for logging. This practice, called tree spiking, can cause severe damage to loggers' saws when blades contact the hidden spikes, either in the forest or at the logging mill. In the 1987 incident, at the Louisiana-Pacific lumber mill in Cloverdale, California, a saw shattered after hitting an eleven-inch spike. Pieces of the saw struck millworker George Alexander in the face, and his jaw was broken. Many people, including other environmentalists, were quick to condemn Earth First! for promoting such a dangerous activity. These critics argued that violence is never right, no matter the cause, and suggested that the use of such tactics would undermine the entire environmental movement. In his book *The Rights of Nature*, professor of environmental ethics Roderick Nash explains:

> There was disagreement about violence even among the new environmentalists. The editor of [the magazine] *Environmental Ethics* deplored Earth First!'s tactics as "paramilitary operations . . . closer to terrorism than civil disobedience." He noted that . . . ignoring [property rights] . . . opened the possibility of a "terrible backlash" and the "undoing of all the good that has been done" in the environmental movement. Jay Hair, chief executive officer of the huge National Wildlife Federation, similarly stated that "we're a nation of laws. Terrorism has no place in changing public policy." . . . Even [poet] Gary Snyder, a pioneer in articulating the rights of nature and an Earth First! supporter, warned the organization that violence against property or people should only be undertaken as a last resort and then only "with a true warrior's consciousness," rather than . . . casual pranksterism.

Violence against property

Nonetheless, members of Earth First! continue to endorse violent activities, although some make a distinction between violence against property and violence against people. Nash quotes a North Carolina member of Earth First! as saying: "Of course we have a moral right to act against lifeless 'property' to preserve the Earth. . . . Such acts of conscience are *not* violence; they are our *duty* if we are true stewards of this Earth. . . . [But] all action must be *non-violent to life*." However, tree spiking and other potentially life-threatening activities continue.

More recently, Earth First!ers have developed a new type of nonviolent illegal activism that focuses on property. It calls this activity "ethical shoplifting," which is the intentional theft of anti-environmental products from stores. Earth First! has primarily used this tactic to end the importation of mahogany, a tropical hardwood, into parts of Great Britain.

The group believes that mahogany logging has been the primary cause of deforestation in the Brazilian Amazon rain forest, and 56 percent of the demand for mahogany comes from Great Britain. Consequently in 1993, British Earth First! groups began targeting products made from mahogany for ethical shoplifting. Manchester members describe the activity as follows:

> [Ethical shoplifting] involves the "liberation" of pieces of the wood from stores that sell it, and then taking them down to the local police station to report them as stolen property. . . . In late 1993, this occurred on numerous occasions . . . in many . . . towns and cities around Britain. . . . Banister rails, towel racks, tables and other miscellaneous objects went walkabouts at increasingly frequent intervals. Eventually just before Christmas, a fax from [a store in Great Britain said they] were going to stop importing Brazilian mahogany forthwith, and merely going to sell their remaining stock before discontinuing the trade for good. We had won!!!

Physical confrontation

Earth First! believes that covert illegal acts such as ethical shoplifting and monkeywrenching are excellent ways

In 1987 a millworker was injured by a metal spike that Earth First!ers had driven into a tree marked for logging. Tree-spiking, a form of radical environmentalism, is a hazard for many workers in the lumber industry.

to protect the environment. It also promotes face-to-face conflict over environmental issues.

For example, during a September 1996 protest against logging efforts in the Headwaters Redwood Forest 280 miles north of San Francisco, California, Earth First! protesters and members of other radical groups blocked roads, flattened tires, lay in front of cars, chained themselves to lumber company gates, and struggled with the police who came to arrest them.

Similarly, in 1996 environmentalists protesting the destruction of a large forest in Newbury, England, built elaborate tree houses and occupied the trees until police arrested them. Reporter John Vidal, in his article "Hearts of Oak," describes the scene before the arrival of police:

> [There are] scores of camps, with hundreds of people in tree houses or in "benders" made of bent hazelwood and plastic sheeting on the frozen ground. Some tree houses, like "the Mothership" at the Kennet River camp, stretch across nine or

ten trees and have separate kitchens and sleeping areas. Others are no more than "twigloos," fragile nests for one or two people in the highest branches.

Vidal reports that the police used giant cherrypicker machines to reach and arrest 778 of the tree house dwellers during March and April of 1996. These forced removals often resulted in hand-to-hand fights, but eventually all the protesters were taken away and ten thousand trees were cut down in preparation for the road construction.

An "unwavering presence"

However, not all radical groups that advocate face-to-face confrontation also endorse violence. Greenpeace, for example, was founded in 1971 by a small group of peaceful Canadians who wanted to block the detonation of a nuclear device in a U.S. atomic test zone near Alaska. Originally called the "Don't Make a Wave Committee," this group believed that the explosion would create an earthquake and tidal wave that would destroy the surrounding area and its wildlife. Members set off for the region in a fishing boat, hoping that the United States would not conduct the test with innocent people present.

Participating in a radical method of protest, an Earth First! activist in California hangs from a tree that is scheduled for logging. He was arrested by police.

Eventually the group was forced to turn back, but its activities brought to public attention the issue of nuclear testing. Other people began to protest the government's activities, and three months later the testing zone was turned into a bird sanctuary. Given this success, the group's on-line literature says:

> Greenpeace today adheres to the same principle that led 12 people to sail a small boat into the U.S. atomic test zone . . . in 1971: that determined individuals can alter the actions and purposes of even the most powerful by 'bearing witness', that is, by drawing attention to an abuse of the environment through their unwavering presence at the scene, whatever the risk.

Greenpeace has used this tactic many times. For example, in the late 1970s, its members sailed the North Atlantic in a ship called the *Rainbow Warrior* to protest whaling. Wherever they encountered a whaling ship, they would launch inflatable rafts and position themselves between the whalers and the whales, thereby blocking the ship's harpoons.

Similarly, between 1976 and 1984, Greenpeace members made several trips to the east coast of Canada, where Norwegians and Canadians carried out commercial seal hunting. Every spring, these sealers would club to death hundreds of thousands of baby seals and sell their skins to furriers. To protect the seals, Greenpeace members acted as human shields, protecting the animals with their own bodies, or painted the baby seals with a harmless green dye to make their coats worthless.

Using the media

While such tactics saved individual whales and seals, they did not stop the widespread slaughter of these animals. To that end, members of Greenpeace learned to use the media to broaden their influence. For example, Greenpeace arranged to have their confrontations with whalers filmed. They also followed whale-processing ships and photographed their workers hauling dead whales from the water. The public found these televised images shocking and public opinion was sympathetic to the whales' plight. In response, people began to donate money to finance more Greenpeace antiwhaling expeditions and support antiwhaling regulations by the International Whaling Commission.

In the case of the baby seals, public outrage was widespread after Greenpeace arranged for a television crew to document a seal kill. In 1982 the European Parliament, an international body that sets common policies, responded to public pressure by banning the import of seal pup skins by its fifteen member nations. According to Greenpeace literature: "Such a blow to the market was enough to all but wipe out the international market for seal pup fur."

Publicizing its activities was an extremely effective strategy, and Greenpeace grew to an organization of 5 mil-

Using the media to gain public support for its causes, Greenpeace has become one of the world's most recognized environmental groups.

lion supporters, a 1996 yearly income of approximately $30.6 million, and offices in thirty countries. At present, six Greenpeace ships, according to its on-line literature, continue to "carry out high-profile actions, and tour regions and countries, highlighting local and regional environmental problems."

But Greenpeace is not the only environmental group that has profited from publicity. One expert in environmental politics, Ronald G. Shaiko, says that many environmental groups have learned to use the media to their advantage. In his 1986 article in the *Annals of the American Academy of Political and Social Science*, "Greenpeace U.S.A.: Something Old, New, Borrowed," he states that such groups use the media and public opinion to "influence the governmental process through distinctly indirect means." In addition, many mainstream environmental groups publish their own books, magazines, and educational materials to promote their views among the general public.

However, critics argue that such publications often misrepresent the true state of the environment, intentionally or unintentionally, and that environmentalists are biased in the way that they perform and interpret scientific studies on environmental issues. If this is true, then many of the resulting environmental laws and regulations might not be viable solutions to environmental problems. The way that environmentalists research environmental issues and present their results to the public, and the true state of the earth's health, is subject to bitter debate.

3

Assessing the True State of the Environment

MAINSTREAM, GRASSROOTS, and radical environmental groups all offer a bleak picture of Earth's health, predicting disaster if drastic measures are not taken to solve environmental problems. But opponents of these groups argue that their pessimism is unfounded and interferes with rational discussions of environmental issues. In addition, each side in the debate believes that the other is biased and therefore incapable of assessing the true nature of the environment.

Questions of accuracy

Environmental groups support a great deal of scientific research on environmental problems. Some of it has inarguably been instrumental in improving the state of the environment. For example, according to Mark Dowie in *Losing Ground*, scientists have been successful in identifying many environmental pollutants that endanger human health, such as lead, mercury, the pesticide DDT, and the radioactive component of nuclear fallout, strontium 90, and the U.S. government has consequently sought to minimize the presence of these toxins.

However, not all scientific research produces valid results. Scientists sometimes make mistakes in conducting their experiments or draw conclusions later proved to be false, and scientific data can easily be misinterpreted. Environmentalists have made incorrect assessments of environmental problems, particularly when they try to forecast the future. For example, in the 1968 book *The Population Bomb*, environmental researcher Paul Ehrlich incorrectly predicted that overpopulation and crop failures would lead to mass starvation in the United States by 1980, and in the 1972 book *The Limits to Growth*, a group of scientists incorrectly predicted that the world would run out of gold by 1981, mercury by 1985, zinc by 1990, petroleum by 1992, and copper and natural gas by 1993.

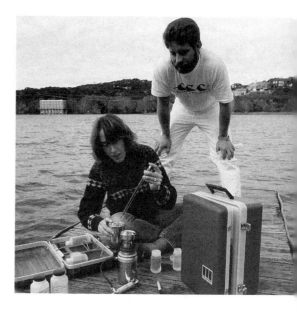

Scientists perform water quality tests at Lake Austin in Texas. Environmentalists often rally behind scientific data to bolster their environmental positions. Sometimes, however, the data is inaccurate.

In *A Moment on the Earth*, Gregg Easterbrook defends such mistakes as understandable, given the limits of science:

> Such way-off forecasts should not be disturbing. They came when little was known about the natural resilience of the environment, researchers having only begun to uncover the evidence. They came when gross pollution was widespread—for example, bear in mind that until 1972 it was essentially legal for U.S. factories to discharge unprocessed toxics . . . directly into lakes and rivers. . . . In the 1960s I never would have guessed how rapidly environmental regulation would take force or how quickly nature would recover, and probably neither would you. So, yes, the [environmentalists] made some nutty predictions in the past. That no longer matters.

But critics point out that such false predictions continue to be made. They also note that these predictions have become more pessimistic. Even Easterbrook admits that today's environmentalists are excessively pessimistic and tend to exaggerate environmental problems:

> Vice President Al Gore has described the U.S. environmental situation as "extremely grave—the worst crisis our country has ever faced." The *worst:* worse than the enslavement of African-Americans, worse than the persecution of Native Americans, worse than the Civil War, worse than the Depression, worse than World War II. George Mitchell, till 1994 the majority leader of the Senate, has declared that "we risk

A CENTURY OF ABUSE RISES TO HAUNT AN OBLIVIOUS, DECADENT SOCIETY!

REVENGE of the ENVIRONMENT

WITH INDUSTRIAL POLLUTERS   SELF-SERVING POLITICIANS   GREEDY DEVELOPERS   AND AN APATHETIC PUBLIC   COMING SOON!

turning our world into a lifeless desert" through environmental abuse. Gaylord Nelson, [a former senator] . . . who is now a lawyer for the Wilderness Society, said in 1990 that current environmental problems "are a greater threat to the Earth's life-sustaining systems than a nuclear war."

No faith in humanity

Such gloomy forecasts, called doomsday predictions, have a history as old as human society. People in ancient times often interpreted natural phenomena as signs of widespread disaster or predicted the future using crystal balls or other "magical" props. Now many critics of environmental groups see similarities between those ancient prophets and modern ones. Science writer Ronald Bailey writes in *Eco-Scam:* "Soothsayers once sought the portents of doom in the livers of sheep, in the flight of geese across the sky, and in the patterns of juggled bones. Modern seers examine the entrails of equations, measure molecules in the air, or conjure with computer models looking for signs of the impending apocalypse."

Bailey believes that these forecasts of global disaster have now "achieved such wide currency and been given so much respectful attention by policymakers and the general public" that "the approach of inevitable doom has become the conventional wisdom of the late twentieth century." Wallace Kaufman, in his book *No Turning Back*, agrees with this assessment, saying that environmentalists "allow only two fates for the earth: the world has just ended or is about to end."

Kaufman believes that this philosophy developed slowly and as a direct result of the environmental movement of the 1960s and 1970s. He maintains that prior to that time,

As they become more concerned about global issues and have less faith in humanity, today's environmentalists often make fatalistic predictions about the earth's future.

conservation groups typically did not concern themselves with global health issues such as air pollution and pesticide use. Instead they promoted public enjoyment of and responsibility for specific wilderness areas, viewing human beings as capable stewards of the earth and expressing what Kaufman calls a deeply held "faith in humanity."

In contrast, according to Kaufman, the newly formed environmental groups focused on human abuses of the earth, and they continued to express a lack of trust in human nature. They embrace the philosophy that "humankind is inevitably untrustworthy and unstable, given to greed and violence" and likely to exploit natural resources "without thinking about the consequences for tomorrow." Moreover, because they lack trust in human morality, environmentalists feel it is necessary to tell people how to behave.

This is an approach to environmentalism that members of older conservation groups did not understand. For example, in Philip Shabecoff's book *A Fierce Green Fire*, Michael McCloskey, executive director of the Sierra Club in 1970, explains that as a conservationist he was "severely disoriented suddenly to find that all sorts of new personalities were emerging to lead something new, mainly people out of the youth rebellion of the 1960s who had all sorts of notions that just came out of nowhere." In addition, he recalls: "I remember being amazed at a meeting of a New Orleans group when someone said, 'Oh, we're not using paper napkins anymore. You can't do that.' I said, 'What's wrong with paper napkins?' 'Oh, that's the new ecology movement that says we can't do that.'"

Controlling behavior through fear

Activists of the new environmental movement pronounced actions either morally good or bad depending on how they affected the earth, and as the movement progressed they became more intent on controlling human behavior. According to historian Roderick Nash in his book *The Rights of Nature*, during the 1960s and 1970s environmentalism "acquired some of the characteristics of a religion. The new environmentalists displayed an intensity of commitment and a tendency to conceptualize issues in terms of right and wrong."

Some environmentalists learned that the best motivator is fear. When people believe that something bad will happen to them if they don't alter their behavior, it is easier to convince them to change. Therefore doomsday predictions became an effective way for environmentalists to control human behavior. As Ronald Bailey explains: "Predictions of doom . . . work. Fears of ecological collapse motivate voters and political institutions to adopt environmentalist policies. . . . Essentially, apocalyptics threaten, 'If you don't do what I tell you to do, the world will come to an end.'"

One event that illustrates the motivating power of fear is Earth Day. Now an annual occurrence, it was first held on April 22, 1970. On that day, Americans throughout the country took part in rallies, protests, lectures, and other gatherings organized to bring attention to environmental problems. However, instead of addressing wilderness issues, Earth Day focused on health issues such as pollution and toxic waste, suggesting that these problems, if left unsolved, would destroy humanity.

The event was so successful that Mark Dowie calls it "the largest one-day outpouring of public support for any social cause in American history." Approximately 20 million Americans took part in Earth Day, and many historians believe that this response was due to the doomsday predictions that environmentalists used to promote the event. Shabecoff explains:

> Many Americans responded to the rallying cry of Earth Day not because of any aesthetic or mystical affinity for nature, to fight for social justice, or to search for . . . a more pleasant lifestyle, but out of fear—fear of cancer or other diseases caused by toxic substances, fear for the future of their children, and fear that the value of their property would be diminished by pollution or other inappropriate development.

This overwhelming support for Earth Day encouraged environmentalists to continue fostering the public's fears. As environmental scientist Fred Singer points out in Ronald Bailey's *Eco-Scam*, the event "showed that frightening the public gets results. We have been hit by one doomsday prediction after another ever since."

Money and attitude

Bailey believes environmental groups use doomsday predictions to gain support for their efforts. He argues that environmental groups "need crises," because "without them, how could . . . [these] groups justify their pleas for donations?" He believes that environmentalists are motivated by money to intentionally mislead the public.

Mark Dowie also believes that money can affect the objectivity of environmental science, suggesting that although "ultimately the great controversies over toxic pollution, global warming, . . . and biodiversity will be settled by science and scientists," people should remain skeptical about the information provided by experts on both sides of these issues:

> It is difficult for laymen and journalists to assess the veracity of environmental scientists. On the one hand, they are presented as objective observers, schooled in the scientific method and expected to seek the truth in nature. On the other hand, most of them are paid to cull whatever evidence

employers or contractors need to make their points and win their arguments about the state of the environment.

But money is not the only thing that can influence environmental research. Emotions can also play a part in the way that scientific information is interpreted. In fact, Easterbrook suggests that environmental groups make false predictions simply because they have embraced a pessimistic attitude about the nature of mankind and the environment. This pessimistic attitude leads them to discount any good news about the health of the earth.

Easterbrook adds that the American public is too eager to adopt the environmentalists' pessimistic attitude. He argues that people should evaluate information about environmental problems more carefully and objectively:

Environmental commentary is so fogbound in woe that few people realize measurable improvements have already been made in almost every area. In the United States air pollution, water pollution, ocean pollution, toxic discharges, acid rain emissions, soil loss, radiation exposure, species protection, and recycling are areas where the trend lines have been consistently positive for many years. Yet polls show that people believe the environment is getting worse.

The Alar scare

One case that illustrates the importance of objectivity regarding environmental issues is the Alar scare, which occurred in 1989. At that time, the Natural Resources Defense Council (NRDC) published a book entitled *Intolerable Risk: Pesticides in Our Children's Food* by Bradford Sewell and Robin Whyatt. On February 26, the television newsmagazine *60 Minutes* highlighted one of the pesticide dangers featured in the book. The subject was Alar, a growth regulator sprayed on apples.

This chemical offered many benefits to apple growers. It allowed them to control the ripening process, so that an entire orchard could be harvested at the same time. It also made young trees start producing fruit one to two years sooner than normal, and it preserved apples so that they were still good to eat up to one year after picking.

However, the *60 Minutes* report downplayed the chemical's benefits while emphasizing its dangers. As quoted by science writer Michael Fumento, in his book *Science Under Siege*, the show's host said: "The most potent cancer-causing agent in our food supply is a substance sprayed on apples to keep them on the trees longer and make them look better." The report then went on to explain that Alar had been shown to cause cancerous tumors in rats, suggesting that schoolchildren who ate Alar-treated apples were also at risk.

The result of the *60 Minutes* report was immediate widespread panic. Fumento explains:

> Across the nation and even in Asia, stock boys and store managers pulled apple products off their shelves and packed them

Some environmental groups capitalize on public fear to win support for their doomsday predictions.

away, and threw out their fresh apples. Frenzied parents, scared for their children's lives, flooded their family physicians with calls. In short order the price of apples fell to their lowest point in years—around $7 for a 420-pound box, well below the $12 break-even level—and remained depressed for most of 1989. Industry economists have estimated immediate out-of-pocket losses for Washington State apple growers alone of $135 million for 1989. . . . [In addition,] a number of orchards, most of them small and family-owned, collapsed and underwent foreclosure.

Consequently, apple growers stopped using the chemical and its manufacturer stopped selling it. Moreover, the government reorganized its approach to pesticide regulation so that the Environmental Protection Agency (EPA), the U.S. Department of Agriculture (USDA), and the Food and Drug Administration (FDA) began to coordinate their activities regarding pesticide health and safety issues, developing common standards and regulations.

Health risk or hoax?

Because the Alar scare increased cooperation among government agencies, environmentalists believe it was a positive incident. Nonetheless, experts now know that the NRDC did not have enough scientific evidence to pronounce the chemical dangerous. Scientists disagree on whether Alar really posed a significant health risk, and subsequent evaluations showed that the NRDC's research on Alar was flawed. In fact, Michael Fumento quotes Frank Young, who was FDA commissioner during the scare, as saying that the incident was "one of the worst instances where statements were made without the benefit of scientific review."

Though some environmentalists now admit that Alar might have been a harmless chemical, they argue that it nevertheless should not have been used on apples. Gregg Easterbrook writes:

Society is better off without Alar. Alar was used mainly to make apples extra red instead of only sorta red, and who really cares about that? Lawrie Mott, the NRDC's Alar specialist, may have overloaded her statistical case but is on the

money when she asserts that eliminating Alar did society no harm. Some apple growers lost value in the crops they were taking to market when the Alar controversy was swirling. But the following year's crop set records for bushels and revenue, showing apples could be grown quite well without Alar.

Of course, many apple growers disagree with Easterbrook's assessment that the Alar scare did not harm them economically. Because the American public panicked over a possibly false environmental report, apple sales fell and businesses closed. Many lives were affected, perhaps needlessly.

Other businesses have experienced similar economic hardships because of environmental regulation. Therefore, many people argue that it is vital to know the true state of environmental problems before acting on environmental groups' recommendations.

4

Economic Issues and Opposition Movements

MANY PEOPLE WHO oppose environmental groups base their opposition on economic grounds, in the belief that environmentalists too often advocate environmental policies and programs without concern for their cost and propose legislation without undertaking realistic cost-benefit analyses.

Growing costs

Environmental groups often fight for laws and regulations that are expensive to enact. According to Dixy Lee Ray and Lou Guzzo, in 1992 the cost of administering and policing environmental regulations in the United States alone was $115 billion. In their book *Environmental Overkill*, they report that as of 1993, "The number of federal regulations [had] increased from 16,502 to 200,000" in addition to numerous state and local regulations.

Ray and Guzzo criticize environmental groups for the proliferation of this bureaucracy, saying: "Who benefits [from these regulations]? Well, lawyers do, expert consultants on environmental law do, and special interests that can manipulate the regulations do." Moreover, they offer several examples of money that has been "wasted" on environmentalism:

New federal rules require the closing of most community garbage dumps and increase the cost of opening a new landfill

Environmental Protection Agency workers inspect storage drums at a paint manufacturing plant. Regulatory measures like these, while often deemed necessary to ensure a safe environment, can be costly to taxpayers.

to $10 million or more, up five times from what it cost in 1975. . . . The rehabilitation of 222 sea otters was mandated after the *Exxon Valdez* oil spill at a cost of more than $80,000 per animal. . . . Dr. J. Laurence Kulp calculates the cost of the acid rain requirements of the 1990 Clean Air Act at $4 billion a year.

Ray and Guzzo add that the cost of environmentalism continues to grow and quote a study by budgetary expert Thomas D. Hopkins entitled *The Cost of Federal Regulation:*

Regulation is an essential but costly tool of government policy. Complying with federal regulatory requirements, however well-designed they may be, creates costs that mostly do not show up in the federal budget. . . . While it is not possible to provide definitive cost estimates at this point, available evidence exists, however incomplete it may be, to suggest that regulatory costs are substantial and growing. . . . The fastest growing regulatory costs are in the environmental protection area.

Environmentalism is a luxury

Many experts agree that environmentalism is expensive all over the world. In their article in the April 1995 *Environment*, Timothy O'Riordan and associates report that environmental protections cost a country between 0.5 and 2.0 percent of its annual gross national product, or the total value of all the goods and services produced by its people in a given year, and that the costs of environmental protection typically exceed its economic benefits by a ratio of approximately 10 to 1.

Such assessments lead many people to believe that environmental spending is a luxury rather than a necessity. For example, economists Robert Krol and Shirley Svorny, in their editorial "Price Pfister Woes Illustrate Hidden Cost of Pro-Environmental Legislation," argue that only the wealthiest countries can afford environmental laws: "Researchers have found that, generally, income must rise above $5,000 per person before countries become wealthy enough to afford the luxury of constraining production [restricting factories] in favor of clean air and clean water."

As a result, many people argue that even in the richest countries each environmental "purchase" must be considered carefully or the economy will suffer. Michael Fumento argues that environmentalists will destroy the U.S. economy if they keep promoting expensive environmental laws:

Some people worry that the economy will suffer as a result of extravagant environmental spending; others believe clean air and water should be a human right at any cost.

> How ironic it is that some of the same people who conclude that the earth is as fragile as a spider's web, that the human body is a sitting duck for anything synthesized by man, nevertheless see the American economy's capacity for absorbing ever-higher taxes and regulations as being as boundless as the universe. Even short of national bankruptcy, needless health and safety regulations can dramatically harm our capability to compete with other nations.

Fumento adds that unless environmental regulations are standardized in every country of the world, American businesses will be unable to make the same profits as foreign companies. He explains:

> It's true that American firms will be able to compete against other American firms no matter how onerous regulations become, simply because those other firms will have to comply with those same regulations. (Although small firms may be driven out of business because they will usually have less

capital available to meet new requirements.) But if those regulation-strapped American firms must then compete with overseas businesses that suffer fewer controls, they will find that they cannot compete.

Fumento attributes the increase in U.S. environmental costs not only to excessive regulation but also to Americans' tendency to "pump massive amounts of money down a hole because somebody somewhere claims to have found" an environmental problem. He criticizes environmental groups for raising public fears and encouraging careless spending of limited government dollars.

How clean is clean?

Similarly, many businesspeople criticize environmental groups for adding unnecessary costs to private environmental programs. In their article "Improving Environmental Management," Dan Beardsley, Terry Davis, and Robert Hersh report that industry participants in an innovative New Jersey antipollution program attribute its success to the fact that environmental groups were not involved. These participants said that much of the cost of environmentalism is due to "the need to deal with environmental groups."

Environmental groups increase the cost of an environmental program because they often advocate standards that are stricter than those of government or industry. For example, many environmentalists believe that no form of pollution is acceptable, whereas industries suggest that some pollution is tolerable in order to bring people the benefits of modern technology.

In addition, environmentalists are often unwilling to compromise their beliefs in response to economic concerns. For instance, in his book *The War Against the*

Many environmental groups propose air pollution standards for industry that are tougher than government regulations.

Greens, journalist David Helvarg compares the philosophy of Carol Browner, the head of the Environmental Protection Agency, with that of John Adams, the executive director of the Natural Resources Defense Council. Browner says: "If you assume there's a pot of money to be spent on environmental matters, what you want to do is be sure the money is being spent on the best return. . . . It seems to me that philosophically where you'd like to be when you deal with standards is the strongest possible standards necessary to protect the public health but flexibility in how you achieve those standards." Adams responds: "We're being asked to give up command and control for flexible management, and I'm not really sure we'll see the results that way."

This inflexibility is the basis of what environmental experts commonly refer to as the "How clean is clean?" argument. How perfect do we need the environment to be, given the costs involved in making it that way? Milton Russell, a professor of economics, discusses this argument in the article "Environmental Policy's Greatest Dilemma":

> To the policymaker, the question "How clean is clean?" is not
> an abstraction. The answer will determine what action is to be
> taken, who is to take it, and how it should be implemented. . . .
> The essence of the "How clean is clean?" dilemma is that the
> successful policymaker must chart a course between the na-
> tional interest of all of us taken together and the individual in-
> terests of some of us taken separately.

Russell believes that environmentalists need to be more flexible in their stand on environmental policies, saying "we should start from what is 'clean enough' in terms of the national interest." He also suggests that if the public perceives environmental laws as being too strict or unfair, they will stop supporting environmentalism and encourage "those who would weaken environmental enterprise for their own special benefit."

In fact, surveys indicate that people do not support environmental actions that they believe to be unnecessarily expensive or aimed at unreasonable standards. Robert Stavins quotes EPA administrator Carol Browner in his article "Environmental Protection: Is the Public Willing to Pay?":

> It is clear, as poll after poll shows, that the public is still
> deeply concerned about environmental protection. They are
> particularly concerned about threats to their health, to the
> health of their children. Many believe we haven't gone far
> enough. At the same time, we hear people saying: "Well, I
> don't know if I want to pay for it. I'm confused about whether
> the solutions that are proposed are really the common-sense
> answer to the problem." So I think that the question is not
> simply, "Are people willing to pay?" . . . but "For what are
> they willing to pay?"

Public support

Often public and environmentalist views on how money should be spent clash. For example, Browner reports that many people do not believe in increasing the amount of money spent annually by the United States to maintain clean drinking water. That figure is currently $4 billion. Yet many environmentalists believe that the government should spend far more on "ultrapure" water systems and enact laws requiring cities to eliminate even the smallest amounts of chemicals from public drinking water, no matter how harmless those chemicals might appear to be. In *A Moment on the Earth*, Gregg Easterbrook quotes one Massachusetts official as saying that if environmental groups get their way, the city of Boston "will have to build a $500 million facility to screen for contaminants that have never even been recorded here."

Critics of such expensive facilities point out that even the most sophisticated water systems cannot prevent operator error. Without careful management, water can easily be contaminated by bacteria or parasites such as cryptosporidium parvum, which infected the Milwaukee, Wisconsin, water supply in 1993 and gave approximately 300,000 people stomach cramps. Consistently "perfect" water, critics claim, is an unattainable goal.

Moreover, many people prefer to purchase bottled water rather than drink water from public sources. Carol Browner reports that Americans in one out of every six households spend approximately $2 billion annually to buy bottled water, which she takes as evidence that "when people have control over the decision, they are willing to spend more [on environmental protection]." Some critics say that this is how all environmental decisions should be made: on an individual basis, using private rather than public dollars.

Wealthy elitists

However, not everyone can afford to buy bottled water. Many people do not have money to spend on personal environmental protections. Therefore, environmental groups argue, strict environmental standards are necessary in order to protect everyone in society, particularly children who live in poverty.

Many environmentalists see themselves as advocates for the poor, who have little or no voice in government policy making. But those who oppose environmentalists call them "wealthy elitists" who do not understand the needs of ordinary citizens. For example, David Helvarg quotes Bill and Barbara Grannell, of the anti-environmentalist group People of the West, as saying that environmentalists are "the

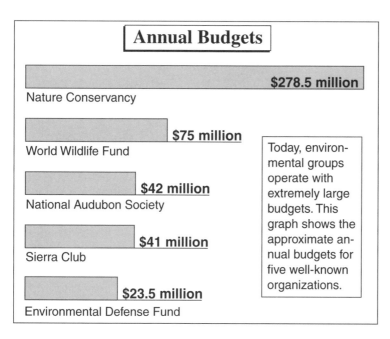

Annual Budgets

Nature Conservancy — **$278.5 million**

World Wildlife Fund — **$75 million**

National Audubon Society — **$42 million**

Sierra Club — **$41 million**

Environmental Defense Fund — **$23.5 million**

Today, environmental groups operate with extremely large budgets. This graph shows the approximate annual budgets for five well-known organizations.

elitists at the top, driving Mercedes and BMWs and telling average Americans what to do."

Such critics point out that the largest environmental groups function much like corporations with executive salaries that can reach six figures. In 1994, for example, the combined operating budget for the top ten national environmental groups was approximately $626.5 million. The wealthiest of these groups, the Nature Conservancy, had a budget of $278.49 million. The smallest of the ten, the Environmental Defense Fund, had a budget of $17.3 million. According to its annual financial report, in 1995 EDF spent approximately $1.15 million on staff, management, and administration expenses.

To many, such statistics suggest that some environmentalists are removed from the plight of the poor. Other critics charge that mainstream environmental groups prefer to address problems related to endangered species and habitats rather than to human poverty, and are insensitive to unemployment that results from environmental regulations.

This perceived insensitivity has been the focus of much successful opposition to environmental groups. Of this opposition, perhaps the most powerful is the wise use movement, which argues that environmentalism threatens the American economy on both the local and national level by destroying private enterprise and putting people out of work.

The wise use movement

According to David Helvarg, the wise use movement first came to prominence in the late 1980s, when an anti-environmental backlash began in America in response to restricted property rights. At that time, environmental regulation was making it difficult for people to exploit natural resources, particularly in areas where endangered species lived. Where work that depended on land use was stalled, workers such as loggers and miners lost their jobs.

The wise use movement began as a response to the economic hardships that resulted from this unemployment, and it has many supporters in communities where factories and businesses have closed due to environmental regulations. As Helvarg explains, wise use activists are skilled at harnessing the anger of jobless workers:

> The wise use . . . response to [unemployment and other economic crises] has been to argue that environmental protection is costing jobs and undermining the economy. This appealingly simple argument doesn't always hold up in the face of complex economic realities, but for out-of-work loggers in dying timber towns, workers in polluting factories being challenged by vocal community activists, or struggling farmers unable to fill or sell off wetland acreage, it answers the question of why the American dream seems to be slipping from their grasp. For people in desperate circumstances whose needs are not being met by the system, wise use has provided an identifiable enemy, "the preservationists," on which to focus their anger and vent their rage.

Wise use activists also gain support by warning that environmentalism will not only destroy local economies but cause a variety of poverty-related social problems. Mark Dowie quotes one of the movement's founders, Ron Arnold, who often gives speeches that blame environmentalism for a host of such problems: "When you come into a town and decide a factory has to close because it violates environmental regulations, you see behavior patterns change. Domestic violence, child abuse, the use of drugs and alcohol all go up to a new plateau as the community disintegrates. Is it the environmentalists fault? You're [darn] right it is."

Dowie explains that the wise use movement has gained support among "the small landowner who is told over and over by [wise use] organizers that the federal government is out to steal his land and that environmentalists are conspiring in the theft." Wise use activists argue that the only way to prevent economic destruction at the local level is to allow landowners the right to develop their own property responsibly but without restriction. They therefore support logging, mining, drilling, and grazing on private land and hold the effects that these activities might have on endangered species as of secondary concern.

Wise use activists also advocate unrestricted access to federal land, both by timber and ranching interests and by individuals who want to enjoy recreational pursuits. They believe that natural resources can be exploited through "wise use" that balances environmental concerns with economic ones.

By espousing this philosophy, the wise use movement has grown in prominence over the past decade. Dowie reports that wise use activists claim the movement has 5

Wise use activists protest the efforts of environmentalists, blaming them for lost jobs and the breakdown of communities. These coffins represent lost timber jobs in Portland, Oregon, in 1993.

million active supporters, as well as 120 million sympathizers. However Dowie disputes this claim, which he calls "an outrageous exaggeration given every known environmental poll taken in America." Instead he believes that the movement is fairly small, with adherents numbering only in the thousands.

David Helvarg agrees with this assessment. He reports that while hundreds of wise use/property rights groups exist throughout the United States, at their conferences "attendance never exceeds the low three figures." Therefore the movement "may be neither 'the most powerful organization this country has ever seen'—as reported in the [wise use group] Alliance for America newsletter (circulation 2,500)—nor the 'brutally destructive anti-environmental onslaught' portrayed in a Sierra Club fundraising mailer."

Instead Helvarg defines the wise use movement as "a new and militant force on the political right that has the

power to impede and occasionally sidetrack attempts at environmental protection, intimidate politicians and local activists, and polarize or misdirect needed discussions over jobs, health, and natural resources." He reports that many wise use groups are allied with major corporations, such as oil companies, land developers, and the timber industry, that would benefit from the end of environmental regulations. These corporate sponsors have powerful friends in politics and the media who help promote the wise use message.

An emotional response

However, some wise use/property rights groups are grassroots organizations run by working-class people who fear losing their livelihoods because of environmental regulations, or by recreationalists who want the freedom to enjoy sports such as off-road motorcycling and snowmobiling without land-use restrictions. According to Helvarg, these grassroots activists often criticize corporate-sponsored wise use groups because businesses are "too willing to compromise with the enemy [environmental groups]." In this way, they are as extreme in their beliefs as radical environmental groups like Earth First!

Moreover, like Earth First!, opponents of environmental groups also sometimes resort to violence. Helvarg reports on several instances where wise use activists have attacked environmental activists:

> Observers of this trend have documented hundreds of acts of violence, ranging from vandalism, assaults, arsons, and shootings to torture, rape, and possibly murder. . . . Simple acts of intimidation—phone harassment, anonymous letters, and verbal threats of violence—may number in the thousands. "Death threats come with the territory these days," admits Andy Kerr, Conservation Director of the Oregon Natural Resources Council, who was told he'd be killed at a public meeting. Lois Gibbs, Executive Director of the Citizens' Clearinghouse for Hazardous Wastes, . . . adds, "People have been followed in their cars, investigated by private detectives, had their homes broken into. I'd say 40 percent of people protesting toxic waste sites and incinerators around the country have been intimidated."

Many wise use activists decry this violence, and Helvarg acknowledges that it is difficult to determine whether such attacks have been sanctioned by wise use groups or are simply emotional responses by disturbed individuals. However, he says that "while only a small part of this violence can be directly linked to organized anti-enviro groups," wise use activists can be blamed for encouraging an "explosive rage" that blames environmentalists for a variety of economic and personal problems.

Sustainable development

Helvarg criticizes wise use groups for the way they inflame human emotions. He also criticizes them for their approach to environmental issues. In particular, he says that they promote a false view of the relationship between the economy and the environment and have confused the American public about the concept of sustainable development.

The term "sustainable development" was first used in 1987, in a report from the World Commission on Environment and Development called *Our Common Future*. According to Tanvi Nagpal in his article "Voices from the Developing World: Progress Toward Sustainable Development," this report defined sustainable development as "development that meets the needs of the present generation without compromising the ability of future generations to meet their own needs." Nagpal explains that this means "we have an obligation to future generations: not to leave them an impoverished Earth. . . . In its simplest interpretation, sustainability is about this concern for intergenerational equity."

However, Nagpal calls the report's definition of sustainability vague, because it gives "no specifics about which needs and desires must be met and fulfilled and how." Not surprisingly, various environmental groups and their opponents have interpreted the term differently. Most environmentalists believe that it is vital to leave future generations a healthy planet, regardless of the economic sacrifices necessary to achieve that goal. In contrast, many critics of environmental groups argue that the most important legacy for future generations is a strong economy. Many politicians advocate a middle course; for example, Vice President Al Gore, as quoted by David Helvarg, says:

> We must not only examine environmental problems through an economic lens but also look at economic problems through an environmental lens, to bring both perspectives together. We have to find a way to generate economic progress without sacrificing the ability of the next generation and the generation after that to enjoy the same improvements and increases in quality of life.

Natural resources are finite. Despite the nation's economic goals, many environmentalists encourage conserving and protecting natural resources now so that they will still be available in the future.

However, Helvarg does not support this approach to environmentalism. He says that "the idea that we can meet our economic needs today without compromising the quality of life for future generations" is an unrealistic goal because "while market growth is theoretically unlimited, natural resources are finite and will always need to be conserved, protected, and restored." He disagrees with those who argue that logging, mining, and related industries can be trusted to manage and limit damage to the environment and goes so far as to suggest that anti-environmentalists have embraced the appealing concept of sustainable development to mask their own greedy concerns.

Many members of mainstream environmental groups agree with this assessment. They believe that through discussions of sustainable development, anti-environmentalists hope to convince the public that it is sensible to exploit valuable natural resources. Helvarg quotes Brock Evans of the Audubon Society:

> I think there is always going to be 15 to 20 percent of Americans who really believe that all these resources are there for us to use and to hell with future generations or anyone else. . . . I guess in a way it's a complement to the environmental movement's power and credibility that we've driven them from outright bragging about their activities like clear-cutting

"If your generation doesn't learn to save the planet, it won't matter if my generation can't read or write!"

[trees] so that now they say what they're doing is sustainable harvesting of timber. . . . So the same folks who always wanted to . . . plunder [natural resources] are going to get into sustainable development because it can't be defined, it means different things to different people.

In other words, sustainable development is a subjective concept. People are unable to agree on the extent to which natural resources, such as forests, can be harvested without destroying the environment. Therefore, as Helvarg explains, many environmentalists fear that "high-tech industrial combines and international corporate empires will use the rhetoric of sustainable development . . . to deny the social and biological consequences of their ecologically destructive practices."

Corporate support

In addition, some environmentalists are concerned that corporations might be using money to influence the actions of environmental groups. Industrial contributions are sometimes answered with offers of positions on governing boards. For example, Mark Dowie reports:

> In 1993 the World Wildlife Fund received donations of over $50,000 each from Chevron and Exxon [major oil companies]. In reciprocation for their generosity and cooperation several top officers of these corporations were invited to join the boards of WWF and other environmental nationals [national organizations]. . . . A 1990 survey of seven mainstream environmental boards conducted by the *Multinational Monitor* found 67 individuals who also served as chair, CEO, president, consultant, or director of 92 major corporations. . . . Twenty-four of the directors were associated with corporations that . . . are on the National Wildlife Federation's list of . . . [the heaviest polluters in America].

Because of such ties, grassroots and radical environmental groups suggest that mainstream groups have been compromised in their approach to environmental issues. However, Dowie reports that mainstream groups insist they are not influenced by corporate board members. He quotes one member of the Environmental Defense Fund board as saying: "Don't worry . . . they don't do much of anything."

But regardless of such assurances, many Americans believe that it is improper for an environmental group to "sell" positions on its board, and anti-environmentalists use this issue to erode support for the environmental movement. Therefore many environmentalists believe that a new form of environmentalism is necessary if the movement is to remain strong. They advocate changes in how environmental groups operate on the national level and suggest that all groups remain open to fresh approaches to environmentalism.

5

New Forms of Environmentalism

Many people believe that wealth and power have corrupted mainstream environmental groups and made them ineffective. Moreover, they argue that the American public is tiring of environmental issues and suggest that the environmental movement will weaken unless environmentalists discover new ways of presenting their positions and generating support.

National versus local

In fact, some critics suggest that mainstream environmental groups have already harmed the environmental movement. Mark Dowie argues that when social movements give way to bureaucracy, they run the risk of self-destructing. He quotes Riley Dunlap and Angela Mertig of Washington State University, who have studied the final stages of social movements:

> In the process of achieving success, a movement typically loses momentum. Its organizations evolve into formalized interest groups staffed by activists-turned-bureaucrats, . . . and support dwindles as the media turn to newer issues and the public assumes the problematic conditions are being taken care of by government. Efforts to revitalize the movement and avoid stagnation . . . may lead to rancorous in-fighting and fragmentation, with "die-hard activists" disavowing those . . . seduced into working "within the system.". . . Well-intentioned agencies begin to fail, typically because they are captured by the very interests they were designed to regulate. These trends

may result in the demise of the movement, as it disappears with little if any improvement in the problematic conditions that generated it.

Consequently, in his article "The New Face of Environmentalism," Dowie argues that environmentalism will not survive unless "rapid and radical changes [are] made in the priorities, structure, and tactics of the national environmental organizations." In particular, he criticizes mainstream environmental groups for "absorbing almost 90 percent of environmental contributions and doing less and less with that money to protect the environment."

Monetary support from the government is often put to the best use at the local level where there is less bureaucracy and environmental volunteers can see the results of their efforts.

Spending on the local level

Dowie believes that more money should be spent at the local level:

A . . . shift of, say, about $200 million out of the mainstream and into the grassroots movement would change the complexion of the entire environmental community. The mainstream would be forced to cut back . . . [its staff], and the grassroots would blossom. Money would be more frugally spent . . . and environmentalism just might come alive again.

Professor John A. Baden, chairman of the Foundation for Research on Economics and the Environment, likewise argues that the money spent on national environmentalism would accomplish more at the local level. In his article "Greens Now Pay the Price for the Excesses of Success" he says: "Every dollar spent on a cause defined in New York and D.C. offices is a dollar less for local problems people can see and feel." Baden believes that mainstream environmental groups waste money on bureaucracy and spend too little directly on environmental problems.

He and other critics of mainstream groups believe that environmentalist sentiment is stronger at the local level than it is at the national level. In fact, Dowie has identified a new stage of local environmentalism that he calls "the fourth wave," which he defines as having "no single defining quality beyond its enormous diversity of organizations, ideologies, and issues. It is part wilderness preservation, part toxic abatement, part ecological economics, part civil rights, part human rights, part secular, part religious, and parts of many ecologies." Dowie explains that the fourth wave has been gaining support because it is a diverse movement that brings together all types of people to address serious local problems:

> By all indications, the [fourth-wave environmental] movement is already well on its way to becoming multiracial, multiethnic, multiclass, and multicultural. It also contains many traits that characterized the American Revolution—dogged determination, radical inquiry, a rebellion against economic hegemony, and a quest for civil authority at the grassroots.

Renewed passion

Dowie sees bureaucracy as the greatest danger to the environmental movement, and believes that environmentalism should remain in the hands of individuals in small, grassroots groups: "What is clearly surfacing within the American environmental movement is some much-needed belly fire and a willingness to be audacious, confrontational, unpopular and unphotogenic. That gives me hope."

Susan Zakin, in her book *Earth First! and the Environmental Movement*, agrees that a loss of "passion, philosophical clarity, and scientific curiosity" is "inevitable . . . in an organization's middle years." She and others suggest that mainstream environmental groups have lost some of their idealism. But some suggest that this idealism will be rediscovered as new members join such organizations. For example, Robert Gottlieb believes that young people will offer mainstream environmentalism an "opening for change, part of a renewed activism capable of undertaking its own . . . quest for environmental redefinition and transformation." Such change, Gottlieb believes, is necessary given society's current political climate:

> We live today in a period of great upheaval, when environmental issues increasingly reflect crucial social and economic choices, and when new opportunities for change are emerging both within the [environmental] movement and throughout society. Such opportunities for change have turned out to be unexpected, broad in scope, potentially far-reaching, and radical in their implications. They involve questions of technology and production, decision making and empowerment, social organization and cultural values. They reflect changes at the

Volunteers, such as the ones pictured here from the group Clean and Green, represent a renewed interest in local environmentalism.

global level . . . [and they] reflect local struggles and victims, as demonstrated by new constituencies and new social claims that may influence the direction of environmentalism.

Because environmental problems can have global proportions, Gottlieb suggests that local efforts cannot effectively address all environmental issues. Mainstream environmental groups agree with this assessment, and argue that grassroots groups cannot function in the capacity of a national organization. Dowie reports: "The mainstream leaders I interviewed often belittled these grassroots uprisings as parochial, pointing to their obvious lack of professionalism, inability to reach the national media, and single-issue obsessions. . . . Mainstreamers still seem confident that with enough money and professional training they can prevail with conventional weapons."

National Institute for the Environment

Others argue that no environmental group, local or national, will ever accomplish as much as the public sector can. In 1989 these critics proposed that the U.S. government create an independent, nonregulatory federal science institute that would impartially evaluate environmental problems and decide how environmental dollars will be spent.

The proposed agency, the National Institute for the Environment (NIE), is the brainchild of a group of scientists led by Dr. Stephen P. Hubbell, professor of ecology and evolutionary biology at Princeton University, and Dr. Henry F. Howe, professor and ecology coordinator of biological sciences at the University of Illinois in Chicago, who continue to lobby for legislation to create the NIE.

The purpose of the NIE would be to identify and evaluate environmental problems, fund environmental research, and support the education and training of future environmentalists. Currently the United States has no government agency that fulfills this purpose. According to the Committee for the National Institute of the Environment (CNIE):

The United States has no single authoritative source of scientific information about the environment as a whole. The Environmental Protection Agency (EPA), and a patchwork of twenty other agencies, conducts research on parts of the environment to form regulations and management policies. Yet no government agency, including EPA, focuses on the science underlying our most critical environmental threats.

The NIE would therefore focus on the underlying science of environmental issues. The CNIE literature explains:

> NIE research will be dramatically different because it will cut across traditional scientific disciplines. Experts in the natural sciences, engineering, economics, and other fields, will work together to find answers to our complex environmental problems. The NIE will be a credible, independent source of scientific information. . . . The NIE's flexibility will enable the nation to anticipate and address emerging environmental problems.

One of the advantages of the NIE would be an ostensible independence from special-interest influence. The CNIE says: "Because the NIE will not make environmental policies or regulations, it will be insulated from the political influences typically experienced by federal agencies."

Funding for the NIE would come from the U.S. government, but the NIE would not operate its own laboratories. Instead it would award research grants to top scientists in academic and private research institutions, government laboratories, and nonprofit organizations. This independent approach to environmental studies would prevent the NIE from developing the interest-group identity so prevalent among major environmental groups.

Environmental scientists and engineers that work for the National Institute for the Environment are likely to be less biased than those working for special-interest groups.

The NIE hopes that by soliciting a wide variety of research from a number of different sources, conclusions would be less geared toward one particular point of view. As the CNIE proposal for the NIE points out: "Whether justified or not, environmental research is often suspect when it is sponsored or conducted by regulatory or management agencies, which have agendas other than that of obtaining the best science. This is similarly true for research sponsored by industry and advocacy groups."

Proponents of the NIE believe that research from more than one discipline could result in more long-term solutions. The CNIE literature explains: "Many federal research programs react to short-term problems instead of anticipating future needs. The federal research system lacks effective ways of identifying and setting long-range priorities and goals for research and education."

The reactive approach

By concentrating on long-term solutions, the NIE would reject the prevalent reactive approach of many environmental groups that tend to address individual environmental problems as they arise, whether on the national or local level, rather than develop environmental strategies before problems arise.

As a short-term strategy, the reactive approach works well, but as a long-term strategy it is ineffective. Lee M. Talbot, in *Sustaining Tomorrow: A Strategy for World Conservation and Development*, explains:

> This approach has been responsible for the very considerable successes of conservation in past decades, but it has little chance of lasting success against the challenges ahead. . . . There is no way to assure that limited resources are applied to the highest-priority problems, rather than to the most immediately visible ones; to establish goals and focus a wide array of efforts; or to establish benchmarks by which achievement can be judged.

> [Moreover,] the reactive approach virtually always focuses on the *effect* rather than the *cause*, the symptom rather than the sickness. If a forest bird is threatened by forest clearance, the reactive approach would be to pass laws to protect the bird or establish a small reserve for it. This amounts to putting a bandage on the symptom of a chronic illness. Unless something is done about the base causes of the clearance, eventually the forest will be gone, with all its other organisms, leaving the bird's reserve an island of trees, likely soon to be lost through ecological change or economic pressure.

Talbot adds that the reactive approach often results in an environmental problem being addressed too late to do much about it. This means, for example, that a development project is already well underway before environmental groups object to it:

> This, in turn, leads to what is probably the most serious problem of the reactive approach—that it is virtually always perceived as antidevelopment, against human welfare. Consequently, it places the conservationists outside of, or in opposition to, the mainstream of human activity, denying them the political, economic, and moral support necessary to achieve lasting goals.

Absolutism

Talbot is arguing for a new approach to environmentalism. He believes that environmental groups need to work with businesses and individuals, setting long-term goals for solving environmental problems at the global level. These goals would take into account economic concerns as well as environmental ones, but they would be proactive rather than reactive.

Environmental activists protest at an antilogging rally in Portland, Oregon.

In her article "Evolutionary Ecology," reporter Lynn Scarlett also argues that environmental groups need to change the way they approach environmental issues. However, she does not address their tendency toward reactive thinking. Instead she focuses on their "absolutism," or all-or-nothing attitude towards environmental issues.

Scarlett explains that this attitude has led environmentalists, for example, to aim to protect all animal species. Instead, Scarlett argues that environmental groups should make value judgments and concentrate their limited resources on only a few important species in the following analogy:

> If, for instance, an environment-loving outdoorsman wishes to equip himself for mountain climbing, he may need to buy a special jacket. . . . Deciding what to buy requires tradeoffs: First, he's devoting his financial resources to a jacket, rather than to something else, and his free time to mountain climbing. Then he must decide what characteristics he wants: how much insulation, how much durability, what sort of pockets or hood, and so on—all keeping in mind the continuing tradeoff between money he spends on the jacket and money he could spend on something else.

Scarlett explains that her hypothetical outdoorsman makes his value judgments based on facts, such as knowing the requirements of the mountains he wants to climb. He also considers the reputation of various jacket manufacturers before making his final decision. She suggests that environmental policy decisions be made the same way.

Scarlett suggests that both environmental groups and the federal government change the way they react to environmental problems: "What is needed is a fundamental shift away from an approach that is primarily regulatory and punitive to one that emphasizes bargaining, improvement in information flows, and incentives for stewardship." In other words, environmentalists should give people incentives for keeping the environment healthy.

Social implications

Scarlett is referring to economic incentives, but others believe that moral incentives are equally important. They suggest that environmentalism be presented in terms of social justice. As Philip Shabecoff explains in *A Fierce Green Fire*, the most serious environmental problems often disproportionately affect poor neighborhoods. For this reason, the environmental movement is beginning to gain "a broader perspective of its role in society," and environmental groups are "starting to appreciate the link between social equity and the quality of the environment." Shabecoff quotes Jay Hair, president of the National Wildlife Federation (NWF):

> When I first came [to NWF in 1989] . . . I did not want the environment to become a subset of the larger social justice issues. But I don't think that way anymore, because I don't think that in many areas I can separate them. If you look at the people who are the recipients of many of the environmental abuses in this country, they are those who are politically underpowered and poor, whether they are urban people who are confronted with urban air problems or lead in paint or the rural poor. If you look at where hazardous waste sites are, they are in politically underpowered areas in North Carolina. If you look at who is losing land across America, they're poor people, not rich white folks. I clearly see an association between environmental issues and social justice questions now that I would not have seen [in 1989].

However, Shabecoff believes that "the environmental community still has a long way to go in the last decade of the century to match its deeds to its perceptions and words, to link environmental degradation and social justice," adding that "the national organizations have yet to blend their agenda with the broader social agenda of economic and racial equity." He believes that mainstream groups need to be more concerned with issues of human rights, and should acknowledge the role of economics in environmental issues.

Forming alliances

Shabecoff also criticizes mainstream groups for their inability "to tap effectively the potential strength of the grassroots activists." Shabecoff believes that mainstream groups cannot continue to ignore grassroots efforts. At the same time, grassroots groups must acknowledge the positive qualities of mainstream groups, particularly the national organizations' ability to disseminate information and influence public opinion:

> Ways must be found to close the gap between the large national environmental organizations and the grass-roots groups whose members comprise an army of millions ready to be mobilized in the war for political power. . . . The national organizations have the knowledge, professionalism, and experience in the niceties and not-so-niceties of national, regional, and statewide politics. They can reinforce the grass-roots activists with an array of skills that can be used where direct political confrontation would be unproductive overkill. They bring their own substantial and relatively affluent membership into the political arena.

Environmentalists continue to spread the message that a polluted planet is unacceptable; although environmental efforts may change in the future, it is unlikely that they will ever be abandoned.

Shabecoff advocates other alliances as well. He believes that environmental groups "*must* make common cause with other sectors of our society that have a stake in changing the political and economic status quo. Potential allies include the poor, minorities, women, industrial workers, and other vulnerable groups whose vital interests demand significant social change." In addition, environmental groups "should explore joining forces with businesses that require a clean environment and efficiently used resources to prosper."

Shabecoff acknowledges that forming these alliances will not be easy but believes that they are necessary in order to protect the environmental movement from its opposition: "Despite its potential, the environmental movement has yet to exercise its strength decisively. Possibly it may never do so. The forces that oppose it . . . have given ample evidence that they will not lightly surrender their power."

Nonetheless, Shabecoff believes that "environmentalism will prevail" because the alternative—an unhealthy planet—is unacceptable.

Demanding a clean environment

In fact, experts agree that Americans will not accept a decline in environmental quality. The public has come to expect a healthy environment, and as R. Steven Brown writes in his August 1, 1996, article "Doing It Better," "The era where . . . governments might look the other way and ignore environmental problems [is] over, in part because the public [will] not stand for it."

Lynn Scarlett adds: "Environmentalism is not, as its critics sometimes portray it, simply a New Age ideology foisted upon an unwilling public. The environmental movement has important ideological components, but the demand for cleaner air and water or for wilderness and species preservation is not that different from the demand for any other good." Scarlett believes that this demand will continue long into the future.

If this is true, then environmental groups will also continue to exist, fulfilling their role as watchdogs for environmental quality. However, whether they will remain in their present form, or adopt new structures, ideologies, and approaches to environmentalism in response to changes in society, is unclear.

Organizations
to Contact

There are thousands of local, regional, national, and international environmental groups, as well as numerous government agencies devoted to environmental issues. Most of them are eager to share information on their activities. A lengthy list of such organizations, complete with phone numbers, addresses, and links to websites, can be found on-line at http://www.webdirectory.com or at http://www.envirosw.com. The following is a partial selection from these sites.

Committee for the National Institute for the Environment (CNIE)
1725 K St. NW, Suite 212
Washington, DC 20006-1401
(202) 530-5810
fax: (202) 628-4311
e-mail: cnie@cnie.org
web address: http://www.cnie.org/

The Committee for the National Institute for the Environment (CNIE) is a nonprofit organization that is working to establish the National Institute of the Environment (NIE), a science and education agency.

Earth First!
PO Box 1415
Eugene, OR 97440
(503) 741-9191
fax: (503) 741-9192
e-mail: earthfirst@igc.apc.org/

This radical environmental group calls itself a movement rather than an organization, and it has no official members. However, it does have many local and international offices, and its Eugene, Oregon, location publishes the newspaper *Earth First! Journal*, which provides information about international campaigns and various aspects of radical environmentalism.

Environmental Defense Fund (EDF)

257 Park Ave. South
New York, NY 10010
(800) 684-3322
web address: http://www.edf.org

The EDF is an organization of scientists, economists, attorneys, and others who work to find solutions to environmental problems of all kinds. Founded in 1967, it has more than 300,000 members and publishes a bimonthly newsletter. It also participates extensively in environmental education projects and helps grassroots environmental groups at the local and regional levels.

Environmental Protection Agency (EPA)

401 M St. SW
Washington, DC 20460
web address: http://www.epa.gov/

The EPA is the government agency charged with protecting human health by safeguarding the environment. It is responsible for administering antipollution legislation and coordinates the activities of various pollution-related committees. It also provides government information on environmental issues.

Greenpeace USA

1436 U St. NW
Washington, DC 20009
(202) 462-1177
fax: (202) 462-4507
web address: http://www.greenpeace.org/

Greenpeace works on global environmental problems and has offices in several countries. Its stated goals are to protect biodiversity, to prevent pollution of all kinds, to promote peace, and to end nuclear threats.

League of Conservation Voters (LCV)
1707 L St. NW, Suite 750
Washington, DC 20036
(202) 785-8683
fax: (202) 835-0491
e-mail: lcv@lcv.org
web address: http://www.lcv.org/

The LCV calls itself the political arm of the environmental movement. It works within the American political system to influence environmental laws and policies, conducts polls on environmental issues, and provides information on the environmental positions of political candidates at the local, state, and national levels. It also publishes the *National Environmental Scorecard*, a yearly evaluation of how each congressperson votes on environmental issues.

National Audubon Society
700 Broadway
New York, NY 10003
(212) 979-3000
fax: (212) 979-3188
e-mail: webmaster@list.audubon.org
web address: http://www.audubon.org/

The National Audubon Society focuses on bird and wildlife issues. It currently has approximately 550,000 members, 300 full-time staff members, and 100 Audubon sanctuaries and nature centers nationwide.

National Park Service
1849 C St. NW
Washington, DC 20240
(202) 208-6843
web address: http://www.nps.gov/

The National Park Service is responsible for maintaining America's federal wilderness areas. It is concerned with forestry and wildlife issues.

National Wildlife Federation
8925 Leesburg Pl.
Vienna, VA 22184
(703) 790-4000
web address: http://www.nwf.org/

The NWF focuses on wildlife and habitat issues. It sponsors wilderness activities, outings, camps, and educational programs, and it publishes numerous books and magazines related to environmentalism. It also provides a current directory of over three thousand environmental groups, agencies, and college programs. This directory can be accessed through NWF's website.

Natural Resources Defense Council
40 W. 20th St.
New York, NY 10011
(212) 727-2700
e-mail: nrdcinfo@nrdc.org
web address: http://www.nrdc.org/

The Natural Resources Defense Council has over 350,000 members. Its stated goal is to preserve the health of the environment and its people and to protect wilderness areas and natural resources. To this end, it conducts research in environmental issues, supports a variety of educational programs, and works within the American political and legal system to influence environmental policy.

The Nature Conservancy
International Headquarters
1815 N. Lynn St.
Arlington, VA 22209
(703) 841-5300
web address: http://www.tnc.org/

Founded in 1947, the Nature Conservancy has over 797,000 members. To preserve wilderness areas, the conservancy purchases land and maintains it in its natural state. It also publishes a magazine on wilderness issues and sponsors educational programs and research in this regard.

Rainforest Action Network
221 Pine St., Suite 500
San Francisco, CA 94104
(415) 398-4404
fax: (415) 398-2732
e-mail: rainforest@ran.org
web address: http://www.ran.org/ran/

The Rainforest Action Network is concerned with saving tropical rain forests throughout the world.

Sierra Club
85 Second St., 2nd Fl.
San Francisco, CA 94105-3441
(415) 977-5500
fax: (415) 977-5799
e-mail: information@sierraclub.org
web address: http://www.sierraclub.org/

The Sierra Club was founded in 1892 and has over 550,000 members. It works within the political and legal system to change public policy on environmental issues. It also sponsors wilderness outings and educational programs and publishes books and magazines related to environmentalism.

U.S. Fish and Wildlife Service
U.S. Department of the Interior
1849 C St. NW
Washington, DC 20240
(202) 208-3100
web address: http://www.fws.gov/

The U.S. Fish and Wildlife Service is a government agency charged with handling wildlife issues. Like the National Park Service, it is under the control of the U.S. Department of the Interior.

Wilderness Society
900 17th St. NW
Washington, DC 20006
web address: http://www.wilderness.org/

Founded in 1935, the Wilderness Society works to preserve wilderness areas and wildlife in the United States. According to its on-line literature, it also seeks to foster "an American land ethic."

World Wildlife Fund
1250 24th St. NW
Washington, DC 20037-1175
(202) 293-4800
e-mail: wwfus@worldwildlife.org
web address: http://wwf.org/

The World Wildlife Fund works to protect wildlife throughout the world. The fund sponsors wildlife research and educational programs and publishes a magazine on its activities.

Suggestions for Further Reading

David Adamson, *Defending the World*. New York: I. B. Tauris, 1990. Discusses the environmental and political climate of the late 1980s and early 1990s.

Richard Amdur, *Wilderness Preservation*. New York: Chelsea House, 1993. Discusses the destruction of wilderness areas throughout the world.

Edward F. Dolan, *The American Wilderness and Its Future: Conservation vs. Use*. New York: Franklin Watts, 1992. An introduction to many land-use issues and laws.

Kathlyn Gay, *Garbage and Recycling*. Hillside, NJ: Enslow, 1991. Discusses plastics, recycling, waste disposal, landfills, and NIMBY groups.

Jake Goldberg, *Economics and the Environment*. New York: Chelsea House, 1993. Discusses environmental issues in terms of economic theory.

Cathryn Jakobson, *Think About the Environment*. New York: Walker, 1992. Offers a clear discussion of the history of environmentalism and a variety of environmental issues.

Ruth Moore, *Man in the Environment*. New York: Knopf, 1975. A well-written, pro-environmentalist companion volume to an exhibition at the Field Museum of Natural History in Chicago.

Jenny Tesar, *Endangered Habitats*. New York: Facts On File, 1992. Offers information about endangered habitats and endangered species.

Robbin Lee Zeff, *Environmental Action Groups*. New York: Chelsea House, 1994. Zeff, a member of the board of directors of both the World Wildlife Fund and the Conservation Foundation, traces the history of the environmental movement and discusses the activities of several major environmental groups.

Works Consulted

Books

Ronald Bailey, *Eco-Scam: The False Prophets of Ecological Apocalypse*. New York: St. Martin's Press, 1993. Bailey, a science writer and Public Broadcasting System (PBS) producer, criticizes many aspects of the environmental movement.

Mark Dowie, *Losing Ground: American Environmentalism at the Close of the Twentieth Century*. Cambridge, MA: MIT Press, 1995. Environmental reporter Mark Dowie criticizes mainstream environmentalism and offers suggestions for the future direction of the environmental movement.

Gregg Easterbrook, *A Moment on the Earth*. New York: Viking Penguin, 1995. Environmentalist and journalist Gregg Easterbrook discusses the philosophy of environmentalism, arguing that environmental groups should be more optimistic about the state of the environment.

Dave Foreman, *Confessions of an Eco-Warrior*. New York: Harmony Books, 1991. Foreman, the cofounder of Earth First!, discusses the inner workings of this radical environmental group and defends its tactics.

Michael Fumento, *Science Under Siege*. New York: Quill/William Morrow, 1993. A columnist who writes about science and health issues separates the fact from the fiction surrounding many important environmental controversies.

Robert Gottlieb, *Forcing the Spring: The Transformation of the American Environmental Movement*. Washington, DC:

Island Press, 1993. Offers an in-depth discussion of the environmental movement.

Frank Graham Jr., *Man's Dominion: The Story of Conservation in America*. New York: M. Evans, 1971. Presents the history of environmentalism from the mid-1880s to 1964.

Noel Grove, *Preserving Eden: The Nature Conservancy*. New York: Harry N. Abrams, 1992. A history of the work of the preservation-through-private-ownership environmental group that includes many fine photographs.

David Helvarg, *The War Against the Greens*. San Francisco: Sierra Club Books, 1994. A journalist and environmentalist discusses the wise use movement and its battles with environmental groups.

Wallace Kaufman, *No Turning Back: Dismantling the Fantasies of Environmental Thinking*. New York: BasicBooks, 1994. An award-winning science writer challenges many of the current philosophies of the environmental movement.

Elaine Landau, *Environmental Groups: The Earth Savers*. Hillside, NJ: Enslow, 1993. Discusses the history and purpose of several important environmental groups.

John G. Mitchell with Constance L. Stallings, *Ecotactics: The Sierra Club Handbook for Environment Activists*. New York: Pocket Books, 1970. Reveals the attitudes of environmental activists during the early years of the environmental movement.

Norman Myers, *Ultimate Security: The Environmental Basis of Political Stability*. New York: W.W. Norton, 1993. Discusses a wide variety of ecological threats.

Roderick Frazier Nash, *The Rights of Nature: A History of Environmental Ethics*. Madison: University of Wisconsin

Press, 1989. A professor of history and environmental studies offers a history of environmental philosophy and discusses current environmental attitudes.

David Pepper, *Modern Environmentalism: An Introduction*. London: Routledge, 1996. A professor of geography provides a textbook history of environmentalism and environmental attitudes.

Dixy Lee Ray and Lou Guzzo, *Environmental Overkill: Whatever Happened to Common Sense?* New York: HarperCollins, 1993. Ray, former governor of the state of Washington and chairman of the Atomic Energy Commission, and Guzzo, a Seattle television and radio commentator, criticize many aspects of the environmental movement as extremist.

Science Action Coalition, Albert J. Fritsch, director, *Environmental Ethics*. New York: Anchor Books, 1980. Discusses environmental issues in terms of ethical considerations.

Philip Shabecoff, *A Fierce Green Fire: The American Environmental Movement*. New York: Hill and Wang, 1993. Environmental reporter Shabecoff offers a fairly objective discussion of the environmental movement as a historical and social phenomenon.

Francis R. Thibodeau and Hermann H. Field, eds., *Sustaining Tomorrow: A Strategy for World Conservation and Development*. Hanover, NH: University Press of New England, 1984. An anthology of articles on environmental issues written by prominent environmentalists.

Susan Zakin, *Coyotes and Town Dogs: Earth First! and the Environmental Movement*. New York: Penguin Books, 1993. Chronicles the history of the environmental movement and the development of the radical environmental group Earth First!

Charles Zurhorst, *The Conservation Fraud*. New York: Cowles, 1970. An attack on the attitudes and actions of early environmentalists, written at the beginning of the environmental movement.

Periodicals

Vicki Allen, "Developers, Green Groups Clash on Wetlands Plan," Reuters Business Report, December 12, 1996. A brief report on a new government wetlands management policy.

Tom Andersen, "Riverkeeper Continues 'Subversive' Course on Hudson," *Westchester County News*, November 23, 1996. Available from www.nynew.com:80/arch2/me611236.htm. Details the activities of a group devoted to cleaning up New York's Hudson River.

Paul Barton, "Fluor Employs Army of Lobbyists on Capitol Hill," Gannett News Service, December 6, 1996. Offers facts and figures regarding the lobbying activities of a company devoted to environmental cleanup.

Dan Beardsley, Terry Davies, and Robert Hersh, "Improving Environmental Management: What Works, What Doesn't," *Environment*, vol. 39, September 1, 1997. Discusses the relationship between economics and environmental protection.

R. Steven Brown, "Doing It Better," *State Government News*, August 1, 1996. Discusses pollution tax credits.

Miguel Bustillo, "Sierra Club Sues Thousand Oaks to Reopen Dos Vientos Ranch Pact," *Los Angeles Times*, September 20, 1996. Discusses an important environmental lawsuit in a Southern California community.

Douglas Busvine, "High Court Lets Stand Dismissal of Suit Against CBS," Reuters, April 29, 1996. A newsbrief report on the outcome of an Alar-related lawsuit.

Ed Carson, "Property Frights," *Reason*, May 1, 1996. A criticism of environmental regulations.

Kenneth Chilton and Christopher Boerner, "Smog in America," *Society*, July 1, 1996. Discusses air pollution in the United States.

Frank Clifford, "Does Earth Still Need Protection?" *Los Angeles Times*, April 22, 1995. Offers an in-depth discussion of the costs and benefits of environmentalism.

John Cushman, "Federal Regulation Growing as Quayle Panel Fights It," *New York Times*, December 24, 1991. Discusses the economic costs of environmental regulation.

Robert Devine, "The Little Things That Run the World," *Sierra*, July 1996. Invertebrates and the Endangered Species Act.

Mark Dowie, "The New Face of Environmentalism," *Utne Reader*, July/August 1992. Originally published in the Winter 1991/1992 *World Policy Journal*, a discussion of the failure of mainstream environmentalism and the success of local grassroots environmentalists.

Claude Engle and Hawley Truax, "The Carrot or the Stick?" *Environmental Action*, May 1, 1990. A consideration of economic incentives for environmentalism.

Maggie Farley, "Condor Conundrum," *Los Angeles Times*, April 28, 1996. Discusses opposition to a condor release program.

Kathryn Fuller, President's Letter, World Wildlife Fund *Focus*, July/August 1996. An address of environmentalism in economic terms by the organization's president.

Lynn Graebner, "Rough Year Ahead for Lumber Mills," *Sacramento Business Journal*, January 1, 1996. Reports on the economic condition of the timber industry in general and the Wetsel-Oviatt Lumber Company in particular.

John Howard, "New Smog Measure Protested," *Los Angeles Daily News* (Associated Press), October 17, 1996. Discusses public dissatisfaction with a new antismog law that targets polluting automobiles.

Margaret Knox, "The Grass-Roots Environmental Movement," *Utne Reader*, July/August 1992. Originally published in the October 1991 *Progressive*, a commentary on the anti-environmental movement and the work of one of its leaders, former Sierra Club member Ron Arnold.

Robert Krol and Shirley Svorny, "Price Pfister Woes Illustrate Hidden Cost of Pro-Environmental Legislation," editorial, *Los Angeles Daily News*, December 8, 1996.

Roger Meiners and Bruce Yandle, "Get the Government Out of Environmental Control," *USA Today Magazine*, May 1, 1996. Meiners, a professor of law, and Yandle, a professor of economics, assess the economic impact of the Clean Water Act and argue against excessive government environmental regulations.

Ken Miller, "Cleaning the Air: Progress Will Carry a Price," Gannett News Service, October 27, 1996. A report on the Clean Air Act and EPA efforts to improve air quality.

———, "Environmentalists Claim Some Wins; Predict a Gentler Congress," Gannett News Service, November 6, 1996. A report on 1996 lobbying activities by environmental groups.

———, "Flush with Cash, Environmentalists Target More Candidates," Gannett News Service, September 18, 1996. A report on 1996 lobbying activities by environmental groups.

Paul Moses, "Wind Shifting on Fresh Kills," *Newsday*, November 30, 1996. Discusses landfill problems in New York City.

Tanvi Nagpal, "Voices from the Developing World: Progress Toward Sustainable Development," *Environment*, vol. 37, October 1, 1995. Defines and discusses the concept of sustainable development.

"NWF Board Member Enlists Minorities in 'Green' Cause," *International Wildlife Magazine*, December 1996. A brief column on minority involvement in the National Wildlife Federation.

Paul Oberjuerge, "West's Resource Economies Not All They're Cracked Up to Be," Gannett News Service, June 16, 1996. Reports on the economic condition of the timber industry.

Timothy O'Riordan et al., "The Legacy of Earth Day," *Environment*, vol. 37, April 1, 1995. Reflects on the accomplishments of the first Earth Day.

Filip Palda, "How Cash Keeps Democracy Healthy," *World & I*, August 1, 1996. From his perspective as a professor of economics at the Ecole Nationale d'Administration Publique in Montreal, Canada, Palda offers an in-depth discussion of environmentalism in terms of money and politics.

Bill Reel, "Cleaner Air Is Worth the Cost," *Newsday*, December 8, 1996. Argues that the Clean Air Act and other efforts to improve air quality are worth their cost.

Jerome Ringo, letter, *International Wildlife*, December 1996. A comment on the difficulty of getting minority communities involved in environmentalism.

Steve Rivera, "Breakdown of Lobbying Activities in Washington by Area Companies," Gannett News Service, November 27, 1996. Lists several major lobbyists and reports on their areas of interest and expenditures.

Milton Russell, "Environmental Policy's Great Dilemma: Is the Public Willing to Pay?" *Environment*, vol. 37, March 1,

1995. A professor of economics discusses public attitudes toward the costs of environmental protection.

Lynn Scarlett, "Evolutionary Ecology," *Reason*, May 1, 1996. Scarlett, vice president of research for the Reason Foundation, a national think tank, discusses the economic consequences of environmental regulations.

Ronald G. Shaiko, "Greenpeace U.S.A.: Something Old, New, Borrowed," *Annals of the American Academy of Political and Social Science*, 1986. An environmental expert discusses how environmental groups use the media and public opinion.

James Sheehan, "Taking Earth Day Too Far?" *Washington Times*, May 12, 1996. A research associate at the Competitive Enterprise Institute, Sheehan reports on government environmental policies.

Barbara Simpson, "Time to Clear the Air in Sacramento," editorial, *Los Angeles Daily News*, September 22, 1996. A complaint about a new antismog measure that changes existing policies regarding polluting automobiles.

Robert Stavins, "Can Market Forces Be Put in Harness to Protect the Environment?" *Quill*, March 1996. A discussion of the economic costs of environmental laws.

John Tierney, "Recycling Is Garbage," *New York Times Magazine*, June 30, 1996. Discusses the pros and cons of recycling.

Mark Van Putten, "Good Environment Means Good Economy," *National Wildlife*, August 1, 1996. A newsbrief on a study that evaluated the relationship between environmental regulations and the economy in the Pacific Northwest.

John Vidal, "Hearts of Oak," *Utne Reader*, September/ October 1996. Excellent photographs of radical environmentalists living in tree houses to block the destruction of an ancient forest.

Lesley Wright, "It's a Dirty Job," *Los Angeles Times*, September 29, 1996, Orange County edition. Offers an in-depth discussion of the Superfund law.

Internet Sources

John A. Baden, "Greens Now Pay the Price for the Excesses of Success," "Risk Analysis Can Further Environmental Objectives," and "Community-Based Conservation Works." On-line. Available from http://www.nationalreview.com. Brief articles criticizing environmental groups' approach to today's environmental issues.

"Earth Day History—25 Years of Wins and Losses," Sierra Club site, http://www.sierraclub.org/.

Michael Fumento, "Greens Still Trying to Salvage Their Alar-Stained Reputation," http://www.abb.org/townhall/columnists/fumento/fume121996.html.

Interview with Dr. Stephen Hubbell, conducted on National Public Radio's "Morning Edition," November 17, 1995. On-line. Available from http://www.cnie.org/. Discusses the proposed establishment of the National Institute for the Environment.

Fred Krupp, Environmental Defense Fund (EDF) fund-raising letter, 1996. On-line. Available from http://www.edf.com. This letter from the executive director of the Environmental Defense Fund promotes EDF's goals.

Pesticide Industry Propaganda: The Real Story, Environmental Working Group (EWS) site, http://www.ewg.org/.

Andrew C. Revkin, "Life's Hubbub Returns to Oft-Shunned Hudson: A River Reclaimed," July 10, 1996. On-line.

Available from http://www.swimnyc.org/p0000401.htm. A lengthy article on efforts to clean up the Hudson River.

"Robert Francis Kennedy, Jr.," EarthBase Celebrity Profile. On-line. Available from http://www.earthbase.org:80/home/people/k/kennedy-rf-jr/index.html. A brief biography of Robert F. Kennedy Jr. mentioning his connections to the Hudson Riverkeeper environental group.

Steve Shapiro, "The Alar Controversy," January 31, 1996. On-line. Available from http://wshiivx.med.uoeh-u.ac/jp/oemml189. html. A compilation of quotes related to the Alar controversy.

Harold Wood and Harvey Chin, "John Muir Exhibit," Sierra Club site, http://www.sierraclub.org/.

Index

Abbey, Edward, 27
absolutism, 67–68
activism
  confrontational, 9
  political, 17–18, 24–25
Adams, John, 48
Alar, 41–42
Alliance for Justice, 17–18
Amazon rain forest, 29
"anti-environmentalism," 22
apple growers, 41–42
Arnold, Ron, 52–53
Audubon, John James, 12
Audubon Society
  budget of, 15, 51
  change in focus of, 13–14
  founding purpose of, 11–12
  membership of, 15

Baden, John A., 62
Bailey, Ronald, 36–37, 38
biodiversity, 22
birds, overhunting of, 11–12
Brazilian Amazon rain forest, 29
Browner, Carol, 48, 49, 50

campaign contributions, 25
Carson, Rachel, 12–13
Committee for the National
  Institute of the Environment
  (CNIE), 64–66
Confessions of an Eco-Warrior
  (Foreman), 8–9
confrontational activism, 9
conservationists, 11
corporations, influence on
  environmental groups, 58–59

cost-benefit analysis of
  environmental programs, 47–50
Cost of Federal Regulation, The
  (Hopkins), 45
Crockett, Kate, 18–19

DDT, 12–14, 34
donations, to environmental
  groups, 6
doomsday predictions
  exaggerate environmental
  problems, 35–36
  historic use of, 36
  reflect lack of faith in humanity,
    37
  used to control behavior, 38–40
Dos Vientos controversy, 23–24
Dowie, Mark
  on corporate influences, 59
  on fund-raising influences, 8
  on future of environmental
    movement, 9–10
  on grassroots efforts, 18–19
  on lobbying activities, 25–26
  on productive scientific research,
    34
  on public support for
    environmentalism, 7
  on social movements, 60–61, 62
  on wise use movement, 52–54
Dutcher, William, 12

Earth Day, 38–39
Earth First!
  defends covert illegal tactics,
    29–31

description of movement, 20–21
ethical shoplifting tactics of,
   28–29
monkeywrenching tactics of, 28
uncompromising views held by,
   26–27
*Earth First! and the Environmental
   Movement* (Zakin), 62–63
Easterbrook, Gregg
   on Alar scare, 42–43
   on environmental cost-benefit
      analyses, 50
   on environmentalist
      accomplishments, 6–7
   on mistaken scientific
      predictions, 35–36
ecological sabotage, 27
economy
   hurt by environmental regulation,
      7–8, 43, 46
   losses due to Alar scare, 41–42
   see also cost-benefit analysis of
      environmental programs
Eco-Scam (Bailey), 36–37
Ehrlich, Paul, 35
Environmental Defense Fund, 51,
   59
environmental groups. *See*
   grassroots groups; mainstream
   groups; radical groups
environmentalism
   criticisms of, 7–9
   "fourth wave" of, 62
   future of, 10, 59, 61, 70–71
   needs to be proactive, 67–68
   public support for, 7, 71
   reactive approach of, 66–67
environmentalists
   history of, 11
   as insensitive to unemployment
      and poverty, 51
   lack trust in human nature, 37
   use fear to motivate people, 38
*Environmental Overkill: Whatever

Happened to Common Sense?
   (Guzzo and Ray), 7–8, 44–45
Environmental Protection Agency
   (EPA), 42, 48
environmental protections. *See*
   regulations, environmental
environmental research. *See*
   scientific research
ethical shoplifting, 28–29
Evans, Brock, 57–58

Fierce Green Fire, A (Shabecoff),
   69
Food and Drug Administration
   (FDA), 42
Forcing the Spring (Gottlieb),
   12–13
Foreman, Dave, 8–9, 27–28
"fourth wave," 62
Fumento, Michael, 41, 46
fund-raising influences, 8

Gore, Al, 57
Gottlieb, Robert, 12–14, 63
Grannell, Bill and Barbara, 50–51
grassroots groups
   defined, 6
   disadvantages of, 64
   how they form, 19
   need to work with mainstream
      groups, 69–70
   oppose lobbying tactics, 25–26
   oppose political activism tactics,
      18
   tactics used by, 22
Greenpeace, 9, 31–33
Grinnell, John Bird, 12
Guzzo, Lou, 7–8, 44–45

Hair, Jay, 69
Headwaters Redwood Forest, 30
Helvarg, David
   on cost-benefit debates, 47–48
   on sustainable development,
      57–58

on wise use movement, 52, 54–55
Hopkins, Thomas D., 45
Howe, Henry F., 64
Hubbell, Stephen P., 64

Intolerable Risk: Pesticides in Our Children's Food (Sewell and Whyatt), 41

Kaufman, Wallace, 11, 37
Kennedy, Robert F., Jr., 17
Krol, Robert, 46

land development, litigation against, 23–24
land purchases, 22–23
lawsuits, environmental, 17
litigation, environmental, 23–24
Lobbying Disclosure Act of 1995, 18
lobbyists, 14, 25
Losing Ground: American Environmentalism at the Close of the Twentieth Century (Dowie), 7, 18–19, 25–26, 34

mahogany logging, 29
mainstream groups
  annual budgets of, 51
  are overly bureaucratic, 60–63
  benefits of size of, 64
  corporate influences on, 58–59
  defined, 6
  have lost idealism, 21, 63
  land purchases by, 22–23
  litigation and, 23–24
  lobbying activities of, 25
  need to work with grassroots groups, 69–70
  political activism of, 18, 24–25
  political influences on, 8–9
  views on sustainable development, 57–58
McCloskey, Michael, 37–38

media tactics, 32–33
Moment on the Earth, A (Easterbrook), 6–7, 35, 50
Monkey Wrench Gang, The (Abbey), 27
monkeywrenching, 27–28
Muir, John, 16

Nagpal, Tanvi, 56
Nash, Roderick, 28, 38
National Audubon Society. *See* Audubon Society
National Institute for the Environment (NIE)
  focus on long-term solutions, 66–67
  impartiality of, 65
  purpose of, 64–65
National Toxics Campaign Fund, 19
National Wildlife Federation (NWF), 69
Natural Resources Defense Council (NRDC)
  on Alar scare, 41, 42
  on environmental expenditures, 48
  founding purpose, 17
Nature Conservancy, 22–23, 51
Newbury (England) forest, 30–31
No Turning Back (Kaufman), 11, 37
nuclear testing, 31

O'Riordan, Timothy, 45–46
Our Common Future report, 56

Palda, Filip, 25
People of the West, 50
pesticide regulations, 42
political action committee (PAC), 25
political activism
  defined, 24–25

tactics, 17–18
politics, influence on mainstream
  groups, 8–9
pollutants, environmental, 34
Population Bomb, The (Ehrlich),
  35
property rights groups. *See* wise
  use movement

radical groups, 9
  history of, 20
  tactics used by, 22, 26–29
    defended, 29–31
Ray, Dixy Lee, 7–8, 44–45
regulations, environmental
  administrative costs of, 44–45
  are a luxury, 45–46
  impact on local economies, 52
  public opinion on, 49–51
  standardization of, 46–47
Rights of Nature, The (Nash), 28,
  38
Russell, Milton, 48–49

Scarlett, Lynn, 68, 71
Science Under Siege (Fumento),
  41
scientific research
  accurate findings and, 34
  on Alar, 42
  lack of, for environmental issues,
    8
  mistaken findings, 34–35
  skepticism about, 39–40
seal hunting, 32
Sewell, Bradford, 41
Shabecoff, Philip, 69–70
Shaiko, Ronald G., 33
Sierra Club
  annual budget of, 51
  change in focus of, 16–17

founding purpose of, 16
lawsuits filed by, 23
political activism efforts of,
  24–25
Silent Spring (Carson), 12–13
60 Minutes, 41
social justice issues, 69
social movements, bureaucracy
  and, 60–62
Stavins, Robert, 49
sustainable development, 56–58
*Sustaining Tomorrow: A Strategy
  for World Conservation and
  Development* (Talbot), 66–67
Svorny, Shirley, 46

Talbot, Lee M., 66–67
tree spiking, 28

"unwavering presence" tactics,
  31–32
U.S. Department of Agriculture
  (USDA), 42

War Against the Greens (Helvarg),
  47–48
whale hunting, 32
Whyatt, Robin, 41
wilderness recreation and
  education, 16
wise use movement
  criticisms of, 55–56
  origins of, 52
  public support for, 53–54
  tactics used by, 55–56
World Wildlife Fund (WWF), 51,
  59

Yosemite National Park, 16

Zakin, Susan, 62–63

Picture Credits

Cover photo: © Mark Phillips/Photo Researchers, Inc.
AP/Wide World Photos, 10, 13, 18, 53
© Adrian Arbib/Corbis, 57
© David Barnes/Tony Stone Images, Inc., 29
© Jonathan Blair/Corbis, 15
© 1990, Gary Braasch/Woodfin Camp & Associates, Inc., 70
© Frank Cezus/Tony Stone Images, Inc., 8
Corbis-Bettmann, 16
© Bob Daemmrich/Uniphoto, 35
© Mary Kate Denny/Tony Stone Images, Inc., 24
© Rich Iwasaki/Tony Stone Images, Inc., 67
© Evan Johnson/Impact Visuals, 47
© Clark Jones/Impact Visuals, 46
© Dewitt Jones/Corbis, 27
© 1991, Piet van Lier/Impact Visuals, 41
Reuters/Corbis-Bettmann, 7
© Jon Riley/Tony Stone Images, Inc., 65
© Bert Sagara/Tony Stone Images, Inc., 33
© Phil Schermeister/Corbis, 31
© Joseph Sohm; ChromoSohm, Inc./Corbis, 63
© Ted Streshinsky/Corbis, 14, 37
© 1993, Martha Tabor/Impact Visuals, 61
UPI/Corbis-Bettmann, 19, 20, 45

About the Author

Patricia D. Netzley received her bachelor's degree in English from the University of California at Los Angeles (UCLA). After graduation she worked as an editor at the UCLA Medical Center, where she produced hundreds of medical articles, speeches, and pamphlets.

Netzley became a freelance writer in 1986. She is the author of several books for children and adults, including *The Assassination of President John F. Kennedy* (Macmillan/New Discovery Books, 1994), *Alien Abductions* (Greenhaven Press, 1996), *Issues in the Environment* (Lucent Books, 1998), and the forthcoming *Encyclopedia of Environmental Literature* (ABC-CLIO).

Netzley's hobbies are weaving, knitting, and needlework. She and her husband, Raymond, live in Southern California with their three children, Matthew, Sarah, and Jacob.